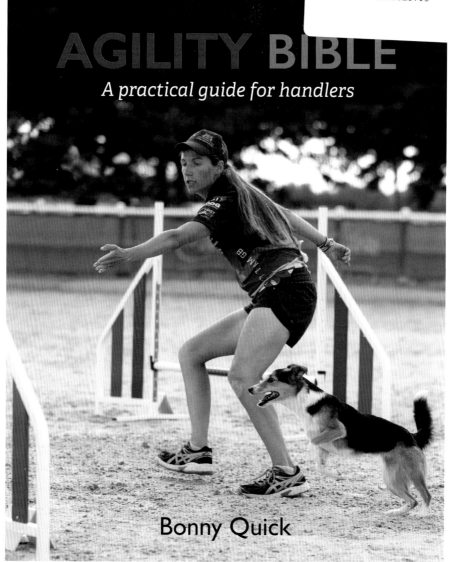

AGILITY BIBLE
A practical guide for handlers

Bonny Quick

PHOTOGRAPHY
All photos by Sean Cameron unless otherwise acknowledged.
Cover photo: Simon Peachey.
Special thanks to Clean Run for use of Course Designer 4.
For more information, see www.cleanrun.com

ACKNOWLEDGEMENTS
To those I love and who make it all possible – Matt and Charlie, dad and Belinda, Granny and Colonel.

To my beloved dogs: Tully, for making me believe I could. Hayly, for showing me what was possible. Ivy, for teaching me how little I knew. Shelley, for looking after my heart. Lucky, for adopting the family. Clyde, for making the impossible possible.

And to my support team – The Win Clinic, Karma Fitness, Four Paws Rehab, Eden Holistic Pet Foods

First published in 2020 by First Stone Publishing, an imprint of Westline Publishing Limited, The Old Hen House, St Martin's Farm, Zeals, Warminster BA12 6NZ United Kingdom.

ISBN 978 1 910488 56 0

Cover and interior design: Alan Cooper

Printed by Printworks Global Ltd., London & Hong Kong

1 2 3 4 5 6 7 8 9 0

CONTENTS

PREFACE

In the beginning, there is love. Before your agility journey starts, you already share a partnership. It's you two together, against the world.

Ribbons and winnings are glorious, but fleeting. No one wishes for one more trophy on their dog's last day. Keep the love you have for your dog at the heart of every step of your adventures.

PART I

THE AGILITY DOG

Chapter One

YOUR DOG'S MIND

"Everything I know, I learned from dogs."
Nora Roberts

A special bond will develop between you and your dog during your agility adventures. Sometimes, it happens straightaway: you fall in love from the day you set eyes on each other. But you are just as likely to go down a much rockier road before you achieve that gorgeous, heart-warming bond.

One thing you can guarantee: your next dog won't be the same as your last dog. There is a reason for the saying, 'comparison is the thief of joy.' Don't waste time wishing your dog was something other than he is. Concentrate on what is great about the dog in front of you.

Albert Einstein said: "If you judge a fish by its ability to climb a tree, it will live its whole life believing it is stupid." Every dog has special, wonderful characteristics; sometimes it just takes you longer to find them. As an individual, you have your own idiosyncrasies. Your dog has quirks too – however illogical they seem, treat your dog sympathetically.

Grow your relationship together by enjoying one-on-one time. Share trips to dog-friendly pubs, snuggles on the sofa, jogs through the woods, outings to the beach, or just finding new walks with enriching sniffing opportunities.

Be aware of how you describe your dog – to yourself and to others.

Be kind, positive and upbeat. Feeling good about your dog is infectious: he will be more likely to fulfil your expectations – and you will feel even happier about him.

One day I was training my two-year-old Border Collie, Clyde, and, out of the blue, he suddenly ran away from me, heading down the length of my venue. What was he doing?

He rushed up to where my eight-month-old son, Charlie, was sitting in his pushchair, and stared at me urgently. Charlie was teetering on the edge of the seat. He had managed to work himself out of the straps was just about to tip forward to the floor.

I ran over and scooped up Charlie. He had never fallen out of his pushchair before, and yet Clyde had been able to spot the catastrophe unfolding and take action.

Allow your relationship to grow and develop.

COMMUNICATING

Scientific research has moulded current dog training methods. You may well be familiar with the Ivan Pavlov influenced approach: reward desirable behaviours to reinforce them.

There are countless dog training manuals rightly extolling the benefits of positive reinforcement so if you are not familiar with the methodology, get reading! Positive reinforcement, along with clear and consistent boundaries, is key to successful agility training.

Rewarding your dog allows you to communicate across the species boundary from human to dog, so that you can reinforce behaviours you would like to see strengthened and repeated. But don't make the mistake of over-simplifying dogs. Just like you, your dog is a highly sensitive, emotional being.

Your dog cares about how you behave towards him. He knows when you feel sad. He knows when you are delighted. He knows when you are a bit grumpy because you are tired – in fact, he probably feels very much the same when he hasn't had a decent amount of sleep.

Play is a great way of opening up the channels of communication with your dog.

Tending to your dog's happiness and confidence is very similar to looking after your own needs. It amounts to more than just meeting his basic care requirements or tossing an occasional treat in his direction. The emotional interactions with your dog are fundamental to the communication between the two of you.

FEELING

If you did some work for a friend, how would you feel if they responded to your efforts with a "Cheers for that" said in a dreary monotone? In contrast, how would you feel if they responded by sounding truly overjoyed, saying: "What a great job you've done! I'm chuffed to bits! How impressive!"

The emotions you show have a significant role to play in the way you reward your dog. Casually lobbing a toy in your dog's direction is a world away from crying out in your most delighted voice: "Wow! That was super!" and playing an exciting, energetic tug game together.

Be expressive. Make your dog feel great when you are pleased! This creates a great atmosphere in your everyday life. Plus you'll make him feel confident, braver, happier – all the things *you* feel when you are genuinely praised.

Of course, the way you show emotion needs to be appropriate to your own particular dog. Be flexible, like an actor, taking on the role that best suits your dog. For example, a more subdued dog that lacks motivation may feel encouraged when you whoop and cheer his success, with a great big grin on your face. However, a more naturally aroused dog, who is easily over-excited, may find that kind of behaviour too much. He may prefer quieter and calmer praise. This may also apply to a worried, or sound sensitive dog. In distracting situations, such as group training sessions, or in competition, you may need to be more demonstrative than usual to engage with your dog.

Think about how you plan to react during training sessions so that your dog is rewarded for behaviours you want to encourage. Ask yourself the following questions:

- How do I praise my dog for behaviours I like – what do I say, and how do I reward?
- How do I celebrate behaviours I love – what do I say, and how do I reward?

Emotions are infectious so share the joy and celebrate when things go well.

DEALING WITH FAILURES

Train clever, and your dog will succeed most of the time!

- Carefully plan and prepare training sessions.
- Prime your dog mentally and physically so he is ready for each challenge in advance.
- Be prepared to go back a step if your dog isn't ready for what you are asking.
- Stay alert to signs of fatigue and stop sooner rather than later.

Inevitably, there will be times during training when your dog does not deliver the behaviour you were hoping for. In most cases, this will be because you haven't managed to communicate clearly enough to him what you want. That's fine. What do you do about it?

Some dogs are fine when you say something like: "try again", and keep your face deadpan instead of showing your usual chuffed-with-that-behaviour grin. Letting your dog know when a behaviour isn't the one you want can be useful information. It may encourage him to abandon the tactic he has been trying and opt for an alternative (see What should I do if my dog makes a weave mistake?, page 126). This can help you both get to the behaviour you want more easily.

Just like humans, most dogs can take a small percentage of perceived failure in their stride. Your dog's resilience is likely to be greater if he is raised in a failure-friendly environment. A failure-friendly environment is one where:

- Failures do occur occasionally.
- The degree of success far exceeds the degree of failure. There are times when you must ensure that a degree of success is almost inevitable when you ask your dog to try again.
- You treat failures not as something scary but as a normal part of the fun.

- You respond to several failures by changing tack or switching to an alternative behaviour. There may be occasions when you need to stop a session, have a rethink, and revisit the game/exercise another time.

As with people, one size does not fit all. For some dogs (or at some points in some dogs' lives) showing anything other than a positive response will not work; it can have a crushing effect, causing your dog to shutdown and give up trying. It can also make your dog feel frustrated and annoyed.

Keep your dog's confidence and motivation levels high. Don't mistake arousal for confidence; dogs can be vocal and excitable but not confident at all.

If you are concerned about your dog losing confidence or motivation, consider this strategy:

- Give small rewards and verbal encouragement for behaviours that are not what you want.
- Give better rewards and verbal praise for good attempts.
- Give jackpot rewards and verbal congratulations for success.

Think about your dog, and his own unique personality. Ask yourself: what should I do during training sessions when I get behaviours I don't want?

The trick is to be accommodating. Try to be the person your dog needs you to be. Show him the responses that work for his specific personality. You will not always get it right – you are an animal, too. You have your own foibles, and you will have good and bad days. However, it is so much easier for your dog if you are prepared to adjust, to be malleable, and to modify your behaviour, based on what your dog tells you he needs.

Your dog's personality is like yours; it doesn't stay fixed, it shifts over time. Observe him closely and respond to him as a developing individual. Read his body language and monitor his reactions so you can benefit from his feedback and learn how to shape your behaviour in a way that can best help him.

CONVERSING WITH YOUR DOG

Think about the last time you were really angry. How did you speak? What tone of voice did you use? What about your body – how was your posture?

It's not just what you say that conveys your feelings. It's the way you say it. Ever heard someone say "I'm fine" and known they are not fine at all?

Your dog might not recognise every abstract word in the English language, but he understands more about you than you probably know about yourself. Depending on how you feel, you will look different to him. You will sound different, and you will probably smell different.

What you say to, and about your dog, matters. It matters to him, and it matters to you because you hear it as well. Want him to be confident? Never be afraid to tell him – and the rest of the world – just how great he is.

Your dog communicates with you constantly. The question is: are you listening? In the main, your dog will talk to you using his body language. For example:

Your dog is saying: "I know you want me to wait here and I'm doing as you ask – but I'm not sure about that dog over there."

How does he say it? As you leave your dog in a wait and walk away, observe the way he is flicking his eyes towards the dog that is standing a couple of metres behind him. His ears will also twitch in that direction, and he may stiffen slightly.

Your dog is saying: "I don't like it when you shout like that."

How does he say it? Look at his ears, they will probably be flattened, and he may be keeping his head lower than normal.

Your dog is saying: "My right hind leg is uncomfortable."

How does he say it? Notice that he pulls to the left on the lead. This means he can keep his left hind leg centrally underneath him and use your weight, on the other end of the lead, to help offload his right hind. When he lies down, you will see his right hind tends to splay out a bit and he often rolls on to his left side.

Watch dogs. Watch them when you are training, in the park, or when you are competing. By building up your experience of observing dogs you will become adept at reading the signs and understand what your dog is telling you.

ACHIEVING MENTAL BALANCE

For agility dogs, the optimal mental state for training and competition is alert, responsive and keen. This is a kind of middle ground. It's a far cry from being totally relaxed and mind-adrift. But it's also a mile away from being over-aroused and hyperactive.

Every dog will have a natural tendency towards one end of the spectrum or the other. His mental state will also naturally vary depending on the context. You can help your dog learn how to be in an optimal mental state.

Where do you think your dog is on the spectrum?

SPECTRUM OF AROUSAL

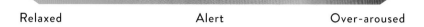

Relaxed   Alert   Over-aroused

If you have a dog who is naturally highly aroused, he will be on the go a fair bit. He may find movement exciting – this could be other dogs, people, cars, shadows. It is usually fairly straightforward to persuade this kind of dog to enjoy toy play. He may be vocal, have a tendency to nip or spin, and will probably show over-the-top behaviour fairly easily. Breeds such as Border Collies and Malinois are commonly associated with this end of the spectrum.

To help this kind of dog attain mental balance, lay down clear and consistent boundaries and focus on self-control work. Make behaviours such as settling on a bed and walking calmly on a lead very valuable. Insist on self-control in the face of the things your dog would like to access. Although toy play can be encouraged, the self-regulation element (leaving the toy on cue and only re-taking it on cue) should be emphasised from early on.

If you have a dog who is naturally laid back, although he may zoom around off-lead, he is likely to be able to relax easily. He may be

The ability to switch off and relax is key to achieving mental balance.

hesitant about new experiences, or placidly take them in his stride. There won't be many things in life that get him over-excited. Breeds such as the Cavalier King Charles Spaniel and the Chinese Crested are associated with this end of the spectrum.

With this kind of dog, the bias should be towards upbeat, movement-oriented games which involve you. For example, make chase play fun. Settling and self-control work is still valuable but needs less emphasis.

DEALING WITH REACTIVITY

Many dogs will at some point show signs of reactivity. They will respond to another dog, a person or an object by displaying behaviours such as barking, growling or lunging.

Reactivity is sometimes blamed on lack of socialisation as a puppy. At best, this is a crass over-simplification of a far more complex issue.

A variety of factors influence reactivity, including:

- **Genetics:** An inherited predisposition to this type of behaviour.

- **Physical discomfort**: Do you know someone who suffers from bad arthritis or some other chronic pain? Do they sometimes seem super cranky? How would they behave if they thought there was a chance you might bump into their bad knee – would they want to keep you away?

- **Accumulation of stress:** Think of the last time something horrible happened in your life. Can you remember feeling more on edge for a while afterwards? Did small things that wouldn't normally bother you make you feel tearful or angry? Observe your dog closely and monitor the level of stress in his life. Stress can be triggered by all kinds of events such as:

- upset in the household
- loud and frightening noises
- busy agility show environments
- a trip to the vet.

Dogs, like humans, need plenty of relaxed, non-stressful time in their lives. They need to be able to chill and switch off, just like we do.

Interactions with people, with other dogs and with the world in general are likely to have positive outcomes if you are aware of the effect they are having on your dog. You need to manage exposure to stimuli in a way that helps your dog to feel relaxed and at ease. Avoid forcing your dog into situations which make him feel desperately uncomfortable.

Your job is to manage situations so they are likely to have positive outcomes.

- **Hyper arousal and frustration:** Arousal and stress are close bedfellows. It is important to prevent your puppy or dog becoming excessively aroused, for example lunging and barking at an agility ring. In the short term, manage your dog so that this sort of unwanted behaviour doesn't occur. When you are away from the source of the arousal, focus on training to improve your dog's ability to self-regulate through self-control games and clear, consistent boundary setting.

If you have a dog who is showing signs of reactivity, your first step is to seek help from a well-qualified and recommended behaviourist. If you have never had a dog who is reactive, be patient and understanding of other handlers experiencing this issue.

BOOSTING MOTIVATION AND CONFIDENCE

When you are training your dog and competing with him in agility, there are many factors that may affect his motivation and confidence. These include:

- **Your behaviour:** If you appear to be confident, relaxed and upbeat, it will have a positive impact on your dog's attitude. Dogs are emotional and sensitive and pick up on your display of feelings. Imagine you had to cross a rope bridge: would you rather be led by someone who seemed a little nervous and ill at ease or someone who appeared relaxed and confident? Be aware of your dog's experience and try to adjust your behaviour in a way that will benefit him.

- **Physical wellbeing:** No one is enthusiastic about doing something that is uncomfortable or incredibly difficult. If your dog is experiencing discomfort, it will be reflected in his commitment to agility.

- **General wellbeing:** Hormones, lack of sleep, poor nutrition and illnesses will all affect your dog's desire to engage.

- **Your training:** Keep your dog's success rate high. If he feels he's getting it right, his confidence will grow. Raise the difficulty level gradually so he isn't over-faced.

- **Your reward strategy:** Your rewards need to be plentiful and exciting. For example, avoid getting caught in a rut and expecting your dog to be 100 per cent keen for a cocktail sausage, when he gets cocktail sausages every time you train and compete.

- **Your toy play:** Keep it fun and, if you need to boost your dog's confidence, allow him to 'win' a good percentage of the time.

- **Your dog's understanding:** To grow in confidence, your dog needs to understand what he should be doing, across a range of environments and contexts. Imagine you are giving a speech in front of lots of people. How would you feel if you knew the subject matter inside out and were well prepared? In contrast, how would you feel if you were speaking on a subject you knew little about, with very little preparation?

- **Life outside agility:** Your dog needs to be happy and content in general life when he is not training or competing. Does he get plenty of chill-out time? Does he get opportunities to zoom around off lead?

- **Your dog's ability to adapt:** You need to prepare your dog for changes in the environment so he is not suddenly forced to cope with something that is new and unfamiliar. For example, if he does 10 simulated competition runs where you make sure he has a great time, rewarding him in the ring and, generally, acting just like you do in training, he is likely to cope better if the 11th run is a real competition.

- **Your everyday partnership:** Have you taught your dog to look to you to fulfil his needs? Has he learned that you will keep him safe? Does he think you are fun and loving?

Improvements in confidence happen gradually. Be patient, and regulate your behaviour to avoid displaying frustration or disappointment when you are interacting with your dog. Review any changes in his behaviour regularly – at least every couple of months.

PLANNING A REWARD STRATEGY

To reinforce a behaviour – to encourage your dog to offer the behaviour again – the reward you offer needs to be something your dog values. Exactly what your dog values is determined by his nature and by his history – but also by you.

In the early days of your relationship with your dog, spend time enhancing the value of rewards you want to use in future. Once your dog has learnt to perceive something as rewarding, it is likely he will continue to do so, out of habit, later on.

ENHANCING FOOD REWARDS

If your dog is constantly full and learns that food comes from a bowl at certain times of the day, every day, from day one, he is less likely to value treats as a reward.

There is nothing wrong with feeding from a bowl on a regular basis. But to prime your dog to value treats, follow this protocol:

- Feed mostly from you.
- Allow your dog to be a little bit hungry before offering treats.
- Be creative and varied with your treats. Fried steak in garlic oil today? Chunks of fish in crispy batter tomorrow?
- Associate a word with eating a treat. For example, say: "find it" as your dog eats. Then progress to saying: "find it" just before giving your dog a treat so that he can predict what is coming.

- Gradually introduce the principle of asking for a behaviour and then giving food.
- Accustom your dog to the concept of treats for behaviours across multiple environments.

A treat pod allows you to provide a more visible food reward.

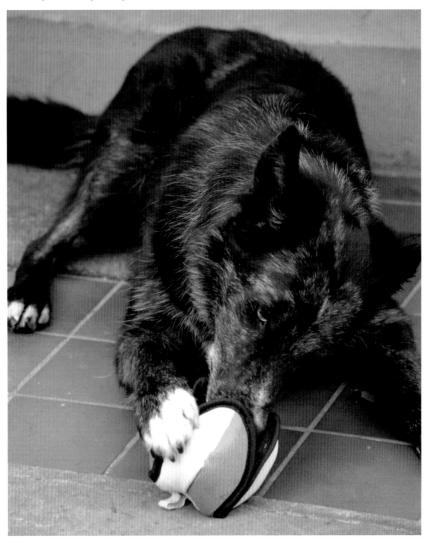

ENHANCING TOY REWARDS

Some dogs play immediately; others benefit from a little encouragement. If your dog has free access to toys at home and plays with a toy on his walks, he is less likely to buy into the behaviour-for-play concept. There are lots of things you can do to help your dog learn to love playing:

- Make play about you and your dog – the two of you together.

- Be energetic and fun. Run around, chase your dog and let him chase you. Make play equal general fun-time, with the toy at the centre of it.

- Avoid waggling a toy in your dog's face. Play like a dog. For example, start by teasing him with an amazing new toy that he's never seen before. When he goes to get it, pull it just out of reach a few times. Then let him grab a corner and allow him to believe he's won it from you. Chase after him, pretending that you are desperate to get the toy from him – even though you are secretly delighted he's running around with it in his mouth!

- Once your dog drops a toy, do not leave it lying around, as this devalues it.

- Experiment with different toys. Some dogs love the thrill of chasing a rolling ball. Some love holding a soft tug toy in their mouth. Some like to bite down hard through rubber and hear a squeaker. Be open to what your dog finds most fun. Go with what he loves, at least until he's in the habit of play, when he may become more flexible.

- Associate a word with playing. For example, say: "get it" as your dog tugs. Then progress to saying: "get it" just before engaging your dog in a tug game so that he can predict what is coming.

- Gradually introduce the principle of asking for a behaviour and then playing with a toy.

- It takes practice to go from great toy play in your house to great toy play in any environment. Transition to your garden first. Then ask your dog to engage with play on a walk with no distractions, then add in some distractions, and so on. It will take time, but ultimately you can make toy play reliable wherever you are.

*One of my dogs, Shelley, has multiple Championship Certificates and doesn't work for a toy. Yes, she **will** work for a toy. Yes, she **will** do agility for a toy. In training, I occasionally reward with one. But if she had to choose between an amazing treat and an amazing toy, she would always choose the treat. When we run big finals, we both know there is something delicious waiting for her on the finish line. Not running for a toy has never affected her motivation, her speed or her all-round ability. Your dog can attain agility stardom whatever his preferred reward. Focus on the two of you having a fabulous time and experiencing great joy at the point of rewarding.*

CHOOSING A REWARD

Avoid being too same-y when you reward your dog. Don't reward with the same tug toy, just because you always have. Don't always bake the same liver cake. Dogs are smart. They learn fast and they get bored fast. You don't want Weetabix three times a day, do you?

Vary the reward depending on the circumstances. Bear in mind the following points:

- How visible does the reward need to be? Does it need to fit in a pocket or into a fist? If it's on the ground, should it contrast with the surface?

- Do you need several of the same reward so you can reward beside you, and away from you, with equal value in a single session?

- If your dog finds food less exciting than toys, but still works well for food, it may be useful when you want your dog to think or focus on you. Food is very black and white. It's also not as distracting as a toy as there tends to be less of a break in the behaviour for a food reward.

- Do you want to raise or lower your dog's arousal and speed?

  - **If you want to raise it:** Use rewards that are highly exciting to your dog. If you are using treats, most dogs love freshly cooked, fatty, protein-rich food, such as bacon. Just make sure it's dog safe. If you are using toys, think about what your dog loves most. Also consider how easily the reward will roll or travel on the floor, and whether that is advantageous or not. You can also use treat balls which allow you to propel a treat a similar distance to a toy.

  - **If you want to lower it:** Think about using rewards which your dog likes but isn't really excited about. For example, you could use kibble for treats. If you are playing with a toy, choose one your dog is very familiar with and minimise the time he engages with it. Also consider using a reward which won't travel far if it is dropped.

WHERE AND WHEN?

Where you reward and the timing of the reward delivery are super important. They determine what you are reinforcing.

Where

- A reward given from your hand adds value to your dog reading your body and responding to you.

  Example: You turn tightly to cue your dog to come with you, rather than head for the off-course tunnel entry. Rewarding from your hand the moment he follows you will make him even keener to be attentive to your body language.

- A static or thrown reward, which is away from you, adds value to your dog doing a behaviour independently.

  Example: As your dog runs ahead of you through a tunnel he sees his toy out in front of him and races forward to get it. The placement of the reward makes him keener to drive away from you, and adds value to going forward into the tunnel, without needing you to accompany him.

When

- If the last thing your dog thinks about before getting his reward is an obstacle behaviour, you will add value to that behaviour.

  Example: Your dog completes the last weave pole and spots his reward landing immediately up ahead. The last thing he was thinking about, prior to getting his reward, was doing the weave.

Build value for the reward, and use reward positioning to facilitate learning.

- If the last thing your dog thinks about before getting his reward is you, you will add value to his choice to focus on you.

  Example: Your dog completes the last weave pole. You fumble in your pocket, he looks at you, and then you throw him his reward. The last thing he was thinking about was looking at you.

Bear in mind the physical impact on your dog as you deliver the reward. Sudden twists and turns, or rapid acceleration/deceleration are all stressors on your dog's body.

DEALING WITH TOY/FOOD DISTRACTIONS

If you teach your dog to love his toy, he may find it difficult to work when the toy is left unattended, such as at the end of a sequence or course. He may also struggle to focus if he knows someone else is holding his toy.

It's normal for your dog to find these things hard, until you have explained to him how to work around them. Try the following:

- Ask a helper to hold a 'boring', low-value toy close by your dog. (If he goes direct to the toy, ensure the helper pops it in a pocket for a moment and doesn't interact with him.) Show your dog you have a much better toy on you and invite him to play. Repeat, progressing to leaving the low-value toy on the ground, with the helper nearby.
- Next, develop the game as follows:
  - Let your dog go the low-value toy on the ground and invite him to you for a brief play with it. Then put that toy down, produce your high-value toy and engage him in play.
  - Encourage your dog to play chase-me games near the low-value, static toy so he gets used to seeing it and going past it.

For example, turn a quick circle around the static toy and let him follow you. As you go past the toy on the ground, whip out the high-value toy from your pocket and engage him in play.

- Slowly raise the value of the toy on the ground, until you have two identical toys – one that is static on the ground, and one in your pocket.

If your dog is a foodie, he may become distracted when he knows there is food around. This behaviour is understandable, you just need to train him through it. Try the following:

• Prepare some really boring food (start with something like cooked white rice), put it in a bowl on the ground and ask a helper to stand near it. (If the dog goes direct to the bowl, the helper lifts it out of reach, without interacting with him.) Show your dog you have a much tastier treat on you and reward several times.

• Now progress the game as follows:

- Let your dog get closer to the bowl before encouraging him to come to you for your fabulous, high-value treats.

- Play chase-me games with your dog near the bowl so he gets used to seeing it and going past it. For example, circle round the bowl and ask him to follow you. Shortly after he has gone past the bowl, whip out your high-value treat and reward.

- Slowly raise the value of the food in the bowl, while retaining a slightly higher-value food reward on you.

GOING FORWARD

With every dog you train, you will experience a combination of challenges, delights and surprises. Few journeys are plain sailing so consider where you can find help along the way, and be prepared to face both the ups and downs.

Chapter Two
YOUR DOG'S BODY

*"Physical fitness is not only one of the most important keys
to a healthy body, it is the basis of dynamic and creative
intellectual activity."*
John F. Kennedy

Agility is an incredibly demanding sport for your dog. He has to accelerate and decelerate, take off for jumps, absorb the impact of landing, balance on unstable platforms while running, turn at speed, suspend his entire weight over an individual limb, and much more.

Imagine for a moment what doing agility is really like for your dog. He dives out of the darkness of a tunnel and hears you telling him to drive over a jump. Even as his eyes adjust to the bright sunshine he assesses exactly how high and how far away that jump is. As he travels forwards he is deciding exactly how many strides to take and where to take-off. Simultaneously, he reads the front cross that you are beginning to cue and prepares to make a lead leg change.

To be competent at agility our dogs need to be fit. To be competitive they need to be fitter. To be world-class they need to be super fit.

No matter how great or small your ambitions, it is your responsibility to ensure your dog is fit enough to take part. Obviously this will increase your chances of success. More importantly, it will minimise the risk of injury and maximise the chance of your dog enjoying a happy, healthy and pain-free retirement.

We ask a huge amount from our agility dogs.   Photo: fotografdaniel SE

FITNESS FIRST

Imagine two people. One is a healthy, muscular weight and enjoys going to the gym, rowing and swimming. The other is a slightly overweight couch potato with a sedentary lifestyle. Both decide to take up 100 metre hurdling. Who will find it easier?

If your dog is strong, body aware, well co-ordinated and fit, it will be much easier for him to master agility. He will be far more likely to be consistent and competitive. And his risk of injury will be greatly diminished.

Be cautious of doing agility equipment-based training before your puppy's growth plates have closed. Impact activities before this stage can affect his development. Plan your training programme alongside a canine health professional, who can help you tailor it to your individual dog.

Chronologically, fitness work should come first. Get to know your dog's strengths and weaknesses before bringing him to an agility programme. It is much easier for him to learn behaviours with the form and the accuracy you want, when he is physically fabulous.

CHOOSING THE RIGHT DOG FOR THE JOB

Agility presents both mental and physical challenges and while training and fitness regimes will significantly improve outcomes, a dog needs the conformation and personality that will allow him to do the job.

There is a growing trend to breed litters specifically with agility in mind. This involves analysing the physical make-up of parents, close relatives, and previous generations, as well as evaluating temperament. Exciting lines of Border Collies are now being developed, as well as Shetland Sheepdogs and Malinois.

Cross breeding has also proved successful, with combinations such as Border Collie x Papillon and Border Collie x Cocker Spaniel making their mark.

Mixed breeding can produce great agility dogs. This is a Cocker Spaniel x Border Collie, owned by Tanya Harper.

FITNESS ROUTINE

As your dog's trainer, your job is to teach his brain and to optimise his ability to deliver via his body. The best way to approach improving and maintaining your dog's fitness is to find the canine equivalent of a sports and conditioning coach. There are veterinary and physiotherapy practices that specialise in working with agility dogs, and their experience and first-hand knowledge is invaluable.

The best plan is to discuss your dog's physical make-up and conformation with a canine health professional who will help you work out your dog's strengths and weakness. For example your dog may be long in the back, or his joints may be hypermobile. Your canine health professional can help you devise a fitness programme specifically for your dog.

Work at your dog's fitness away from agility.

A typical programme might include:

- Regular daily exercise, both off lead and on lead.
- Physiotherapy.
- Massage and other recovery techniques.
- Hydrotherapy.
- Core, balance and proprioception exercises.
- Jogging.
- Sprint sets.
- Rest.
- Flexibility work.
- Nutrition advice.

Anytime you step up your dog's exercise routine, do so gradually.

PHYSICAL WARNING SIGNS

A dog's mental and physical states are intertwined. A dog who seems to lack motivation or under-performs may be emotionally unsettled. But he may also be lacking in fitness or carrying an injury.

Signs of physical discomfort may present in other ways which are just as easy to misinterpret. A dog that is over-aroused or seems manic may be expressing frustration at his body's inability to perform the required behaviours.

Signs of physical discomfort include:

- Appearing disinterested, including avoidance behaviours, such as zoomies or sniffing.
- A decrease in pace.
- Excessive barking or other vocalising.

- Spinning, for example before obstacles.
- A reluctance to move off the start-line.
- Speeding up as the course progresses.
- Inconsistent enthusiasm (great on one run, poor on another).
- Inconsistent performance of a behaviour, such as the weaves.
- A drop in performance – for example, starting to take more poles.
- A drop in speed on a piece of equipment, or generally.
- Struggling with a particular behaviour – such as slicing a jump or decelerating to a two-on, two-off.
- Performing better in one direction than the other – for example, turning tight better to the left than the right.

Be vigilant, and organise a health check if you have any concerns regarding your dog's physical wellbeing.

Your dog cannot use words to tell you how he is feeling. Avoid assuming that repetitive pole knocking just needs correcting, or that commonly overshooting the weave entry is simply excess enthusiasm. Equally, running around at speed on walks cannot be interpreted as a green light for physical wellbeing.

While there are hormonal and psychological factors that can lead to poor motivation and over-arousal, your first port of call should be to organise a thorough physical health check. Bear in mind, not every local vet is accustomed to agility dogs. An elite tennis player is unlikely go to a general doctor to treat an injury. Equally, an agility dog needs the expertise of a qualified canine health professional who has relevant experience in the sport.

ACUTE INJURIES

Unexpected events sometimes happen while training or competing at agility. A dog can fall off a dog-walk, stumble in a tunnel, or hit a jump pole awkwardly. Fitness can both reduce the occurrence of these events and make recovery from them quicker.

When anything untoward happens the best way to respond is to stop immediately, even if the dog appears to be fine. Immediate treatments such as rest, ice and anti-inflammatories can be useful – but it's always best to seek advice from your canine fitness professional.

PREVENTING INJURY

At some point in your life you will have experienced pain or discomfort. Maybe you had a sore calf muscle or a twinge in your lower back? You probably reduced your physical activity and rested up for a few days.

Your dog cannot tell you, in words, when he's going through that kind of experience. If it isn't detected quickly he will, likely, continue to run, train and compete, and exacerbate the injury. You therefore need to be on the lookout so that you can spot trouble at the earliest stage.

It's less a case of – will my dog ever be injured? And more a case of – when my dog picks up an injury, how quickly will I notice? If you are fine-tuned to pick up subtle signs that tell you something is not 100 per cent, you will be ready take action before the injury worsens.

To do this, familiarise yourself with your dog's normal patterns of behaviour so that you can spot minute changes. For example:

- How does your dog normally sit?
- How does he normally lie down? Are his legs all tucked fully underneath him, or do any point outwards?
- How does he normally stand?
- What are his gait patterns?
- What does he normally look like? What does his coat look like? What is his customary tail position?

It is helpful to take photos of your dog in a stand, sit and down, and to video his normal patterns of movement, which you can then use as a reference.

All agility dogs, including those who appear to be fully fit, benefit from being regularly reviewed by a health professional. If possible, video your dog doing agility, especially slow-motion footage of behaviours such as weaving, and take them to your appointment.

Regular check-ups, plus knowledge of your dog's 'normal' behaviours, seen alongside changes in performance, help you pick up the inevitable niggles that every sports dog will experience. You can then take appropriate action before a minor issue becomes a

If you are familiar with your dog's normal posture and gait patterns, you will be able to spot trouble at an early stage.

full-blown problem. By attending to your dog's physical needs in this way, he will not only be a happier individual, but also better able to fulfil his role as a fit, capable, successful agility partner.

WARM UPS AND COOL DOWNS

Warm ups and cool downs are great before and after any vigorous exercise, including agility. Enlist the help of your health professional to devise a programme that is suitable for your dog.

Tips for warm up routines

- Go slow to fast, gradually increasing the speed of movement. Add in some changes of pace.

- Ask your canine fitness professional about how to incorporate a range of motion exercises.

- Incorporate some mind-to-muscle connection exercises cued by you. Examples include asking your dog to turn left or right, as indicated by you.

- Consider the mental side of things: what arousal level do you want your dog to achieve pre-agility? With a naturally aroused dog, for example, it might be better to finish your warm up with self-control exercises.

- A longer warm up may be needed in particular circumstances, such as with an older dog or a dog returning to fitness, or if it is cold.

- Near the end of the warm up include some explosive movements such as short bursts of sprinting and some jump work.

Tips for cool down routines

- Go from fast to slow – decreasing your dog's speed of movement and lowering his heart rate.

- Discuss incorporating gentle stretches, massage or ice therapy with your canine fitness professional.

- Nutrition and rehydration are important in the first phases of post agility recovery. Take advice on what and when to give your dog after intense exercise.

Design a warm up that suits the needs of your own, particular dog.

PART II

THE PARTNERSHIP

Chapter Three
AGILITY-READY SKILLS

"The key is not the will to win. Everybody has that. It is the will to prepare to win that is important."

Bobby Knight

It is much easier to work on agility skills with your dog once you have mastered some general life skills together. Investing time and energy in these gives you the perfect starting block from which to launch your agility career.

The games and exercises that follow will help you and your dog become a team. While having fun, your dog will learn how to acquire information. Best of all, they will strengthen the most important thing – the bond you two have together.

Remember that when you are working with a youngster, repetitions should always be kept to a minimum. Many of these exercises are challenging for a puppy – both physically and mentally. Introduce behaviours incrementally and maintain a high success rate. Treat occasional failures as a normal part of the fun and to be expected.

RECALL

Train at least two recall cues – an everyday recall, and an emergency recall.

Everyday Recall

This will be in frequent use. Maintain a reward rate of at least 60 per cent. Your everyday recall will sometimes be followed up by something your dog considers tedious, such as going on a lead.

When to use it

- On a walk when you want your dog to come to you for some purpose.
- Around the house and in general, day-to-day circumstances.

Keep recalls fun, and rehearse them frequently.

Emergency Recall

The emergency recall is the one to use when you need a guaranteed response. Achieving a successful emergency recall comes from thinking of it not as a way to get your dog to you, but as a way for you to alert your dog that the best thing ever is about to happen!

Every time you use the emergency cue – 100 per cent of the time – it must result in something your dog considers to be absolutely amazing in his life. Avoid pairing it with anything your dog might consider not fun, such as going on a lead, except in a genuine emergency.

Do not tell other people your emergency recall cue. Never use a word such as the dog's name, so that others do not diminish this important cue by inadvertently using it without rewarding.

When to use it

Your emergency recall will be in less frequent use than your everyday recall. This is the recall to use when your dog spots a squirrel heading towards a road. Or when you are at the beach and notice a dog heading over whose body language isn't friendly.

The other time to use this recall is to train it. For example, use it when you have an amazing, surprise reward such as a new toy or a big piece of freshly cooked steak. In this way you can regularly add value to the word, so it works when you need it.

How to train your recalls

Your dog is reliant on you for many of his basic needs, and food probably comes top of the agenda. From the outset, pair his desire for food with your recall cues. Instead of feeding all his rations from a bowl, feed him some of his food after giving your recall cue. Soon he will learn that it's an important cue to listen out for. If your dog loves interactive play, you can associate the thrill of playing with you (or anything else he finds enjoyable) with his recall cue.

At first, work on getting the recall super-strong in your home environment – house and garden. As your dog become familiar with and responsive to your recall cues, gradually raise the stakes in terms of distractions:

- Can your dog recall while another family member makes dinner?
- Can he recall while someone else wiggles a toy on the floor?
- Can he recall past someone holding out a biscuit?
- Can he recall on a walk with no other dogs or people around?
- Can he recall when other dogs are present?

Bear in mind two points when training your dog his recall:

1. Do not rehearse failure. Your recall will become stronger as your dog becomes accustomed to responding to the cue, as responding will be a habit. Avoid using your cue in a situation where it's unlikely to get the response. For example, initially ask your dog to recall only after he's finished a vigorous game of chase with another dog – asking mid-game will probably teach him to be deaf to your cue.

2. Make sure you increase distractions very gradually, always ensuring a high rate of success.

These two principles apply when training many other behaviours to your dog.

I was giving a training camp one summer near Bristol. Walking my dogs after training had finished for the day, I paused by a neighbouring field, noticing a small flock of rare-breed sheep being worked. Within a matter of seconds, I realised one of my dogs had slipped under the gate and she was doing the 'working'. I shouted my emergency recall – she turned and came racing back towards me – and the sheep returned to grazing.

My emergency recall cue is super strong because I **always** reward it. So, even in this emergency situation, I had to reinforce her brilliant response. Fortunately, I found a hedgerow of blackberries and picked out all the juiciest ones for her.

WAYS TO REWARD

The way you reward impacts on every aspect of your dog's training. These games prepare your dog for all sorts of different reward patterns which you can then use later during his agility training.

As you deliver rewards, stay aware of your dog's movement. When tugging with your dog, for instance, try to keep his spine fairly neutral, with normal head carriage.

PLAY WITH A TOY, EAT A TREAT

If your dog gets in the habit of easily exchanging from a toy to a treat, you will avoid issues in the future where working with one in a session means you then cannot work with the other.

Initially, you may find it takes a bit of time to convince your dog to play straight after eating, or vice versa. With practice, this will improve.

If your dog prefers treats to toys, start out with a low-value treat (kibble, for example) and a high-value toy (a new, squeaky, fluffy toy). If he prefers toys, use a very exciting treat, such as freshly cooked liver, and an everyday toy.

This is what to do:

- Give your dog a treat, and then put all treats out of sight.
- Pause for a couple of minutes, and then tempt him to play with a toy.
- Remove the toy from sight.
- Pause for a few minutes and then give him a treat.
- Keep repeating the above, gradually reducing the duration of the pauses until your dog is doing a direct swap.

RUN TO A STATIC TOY

For your future agility equipment work, it's really useful if your dog will send well to a toy that is static. Instinctively, dogs are more interested in moving toys, but they soon learn that still toys are fun, too! Start working on this skill once your dog already loves engaging with a moving toy.

This is what to do:

- Hold on to your dog by his harness, or restrain him by holding your hands across his chest
- Throw the toy a few metres, and immediately let go of him so he can go to his reward.
- Invite him to you for a game with the toy.
- Repeat the above, gradually lengthening the time between the toy landing and releasing him, until he is waiting up to 10 seconds or so.

TOY SWAP

The toy swap exercise gets your dog accustomed to dropping a toy – leaving one toy becomes the fun trigger to get another toy! Toy swapping also teaches your dog that the best part of toy play involves you.

This is what to do:

- Toss a relatively boring toy a few metres, and let your dog go after it.
- Produce a more exciting toy and encourage him to play with you, so that he chooses to leave the toy he has already.

Toy swapping is a positive experience and teaches your dog that the fun is always with you!

RETRIEVE

Once your dog has strong toy play and is good at holding on to a toy, you are ready to teach him how to retrieve it and then leave it. This will simplify all the training you do with toys further down the line.

Carefully select the toy you will use. It shouldn't be a toy your dog can have too much fun with all on his own. It is often better to avoid toys he can shred or fit entirely in his mouth.

This is what to do:

- Choose a small, enclosed familiar area, with minimum distractions and throw the toy.
- Allow your dog to get the toy and wait patiently until he naturally loses interest and drops it. This may take some time in the early stages. Be patient.

45

- Slowly take hold of the toy. Don't dive or grab at it, or you may prompt your dog to move in on it. Then toss it for your dog again. The throwing action should reignite his interest.

- Once again, wait until he drops the toy. Don't ask or encourage him to drop it.

- After a few sessions, your dog should start to learn the pattern. If the action of throwing the toy is more exciting than playing with it on his own, he will gradually want to drop it so you can throw it for him again.

- Once your dog is predictably dropping the toy, you can add a 'leave it' cue.

- Gradually progress to working in a bigger room, then in the garden, slowly building up the level of distraction.

- You can add in a brief game of tug at the point your dog comes to you with the toy. However, this may increase his desire to hold on to it so you will need to pause the game for a few moments to allow him to release the toy.

CLOSE CONTACT

This simple exercise gets your dog used to being handled and restrained. It's essential for future trips to a canine health professional and for workshops where the trainer may be holding on to your dog.

This is what to do:

- When your dog is in a calm mood, gently touch him all over his body. Also hold him, with minimal tension, by his collar or his harness for very short periods of time. You need to be slow and gentle in your approach so your dog stays still and calm. With most dogs this is relatively straightforward, but some dogs are more sensitive, so take your time building up, step-by-step, if necessary. You can use rewards – deliver them when your dog is fairly static and avoid rewards which arouse your dog.

- Once your dog finds the first step easy, progress the game by inviting a friend or two to handle him in the same way as you have been doing. As usual, observe his body language and look for him seeming relaxed and calm during the interaction. Back off if he is at all concerned.

STATIC POSITIONS

Teaching the static positions of sit, stand and down has multiple applications in your agility training. Movements between the positions are useful for future fitness exercises. It's also helpful for your dog to learn how to be still – a behaviour he will need on the start-line and at the end of the seesaw, for example.

This is what to do:

- You can introduce these positions to your dog by luring or shaping.

- Initially, work on each behaviour separately, and do not add a verbal cue until the behaviour is established.

- Stand can be a harder behaviour to hone than sit or down, so it may be easier to capture a static, square stand initially, using targets such as two mats or two low, wide, blocks. Once your dog gets the hang of the behaviour, these can be faded.

- From the outset, incorporate a 'release' into static behaviours. At first, this just means associating a finishing word with the moment your dog happens to move from the position. You can then work towards encouraging him to remain in position until you give the finishing cue. Do this by delivering a reward every few seconds for a period, and asking your dog for the required position if he starts to move.

You can use a target, such as two low, wide blocks, to teach the stand.

- During position work, use your rewards to add value to your dog being static. Discourage movement and creeping forward by making sure rewards are delivered to your dog, rather than allowing him to stretch forward for them.

It is preferable for your dog to learn a square sit, down and stand. These are positions your dog is likely to be asked to perform many times over his lifetime – being balanced in them helps him learn to use his body in a balanced way, generally.

Once your dog has mastered the general concept of each position, reward and reinforce him for being square. If he offers a sloppy position, release him and ask him to repeat the behaviour before you reward. For example, if your dog rolls over on to one hip during a down, encourage him to move and try again, waiting for him to achieve an evenly balanced position before reinforcing.

Reward and reinforce a 'perfect' square sit.

Consult a canine health professional if your dog struggles to stand/down/sit square. Remember, you should only expect your dog to hold the position for a short period of time.

Progressions

- Work on transitions between the behaviours, such as sit to down and down to stand. Aim to minimise movement during the transitions. For example, can your dog do a down-stand-down without any significant change in paw placement?

- Observe and familiarise yourself with how your dog uses his body, as some transitions will be easier than others depending on his age and physique.

- Increase the distance between you and your dog when you are asking for transitions. You may find that using targets or blocks, which give your dog a specific place to perform the behaviour, make it easier in the initial stages. Keep returning to your dog to reward him in position.

WAITS

This game is the foundation of your start-line wait – a behaviour you are going to use nearly every time you step on to an agility course with your dog.

The wait game is a graduation from the exercise on the static positions of sit/down/stand. Teach those positions and do the progressions for them first, before moving on to the wait game. Begin by training your wait away from any agility equipment.

This is what to do:

- Ask your dog for a sit/down/stand.

- Move a step or so away from your dog and slowly place a reward on the floor. This could be a toy or an easily visible treat.

- If your dog moves, make the reward inaccessible by lifting it out of the way. Then ask your dog to return to his original position and repeat.

- Once your dog remains static, and the reward has been down on the floor for at least a few seconds, give your release cue and allow him to get his reward.

It is all too easy to unconsciously add a facial expression or movement to your release cue – for instance, lurching forward or giving a hand gesture. Be aware of your body language so you teach the cue you want – usually, a word.

- Once your dog is really good at the game, you can add a wait cue which initiates the behaviour.

- During a training session, you can mix things up by rehearsing the behaviour – but without providing a visible reward. Shortly after you release your dog, produce his reward. Keep alternating and he will soon learn to do the behaviour regardless of whether a reward is in sight.

Progressions

- Vary the length of time your dog waits.

- Vary the location.

- Vary the distance you move away from your dog.

- Rehearse the wait in a more distracting environment – such as one where other dogs are present. Ultimately, you will need to practise around agility, in an environment which closely mimics the start line of a competition.

- While your dog waits, make some (non-release) gestures and movements with your body. Wait a few seconds and then give your release cue. This proofs your dog to ignore irrelevant movements

- While your dog waits, say some (non-release) words. Wait a few seconds and then give your release cue. This proofs your dog to ignore irrelevant words.

Increase the challenge incrementally so your dog learns a rock-solid wait in all situations.

Consistency is key when you take your wait to agility. Keep a peripheral eye on your dog up until the moment that you release him so you can confirm he has waited in position until you give your release cue.

When Hayly (my first Collie x Kelpie) was four years old, I took her down to a prize giving to collect her rosette and cheer on my friends' successes. I asked her to lie down and wait and enjoyed the celebrations. Half an hour later, having been to a stall for coffee and popped over to a friend's camping pitch, I suddenly realised that I had left her where the presentations had been. I raced back to find her still in the same position.

AT EASE

Over a period of time, introduce your dog to a range of different environments. That might be a pub, a train or a city street. Watch your dog closely, reading his body language to see how he is reacting. The aim is for him learn to be at ease, calm and relaxed in all situations. You don't want him to be either bouncy and bullish, or fearful and nervous.

Don't pressure your dog, or expect him to love every new environment straightaway. Be patient and make it enjoyable – for example, take a chew and allow him to gnaw it while you sit quietly alongside him.

SETTLING

Learning to settle is beneficial to all dogs, but especially for dogs who will be exposed to the excitement and stress of an agility environment. For dogs who are easily aroused, learning self-control at an early stage is key to becoming well-adjusted, calm, unreactive and successful agility dogs.

Later down the line, this behaviour will make it easier for you to manage your dog at events like training days and competitions. In learning to settle, your dog will learn how to curb his excitement to a level where he can still process information and therefore be accurate and responsive when he is running agility sequences with you.

This is what to do:

To teach your dog to settle, you need to use something that has very clearly defined borders such as a raised bed or a crate.

- Shape your dog to get on to the bed or into the crate in the following stages:

- Wait for him to interact in some way with the bed/crate (for example by looking at it) then reward.

- Hold out for your dog moving toward or making contact with the bed/crate, and reward.

- Progress to your dog getting on to the bed or into the crate for his reward. Keep it simple, by not demanding a sit or a down; four paws on the bed, or inside the crate warrants a reward.

- At this stage, the pattern to adopt is: reward… pause… reward again on the bed/ in the crate. This will encourage your dog to want to remain in position.

- Gradually, introduce a release cue which marks the finish of the behaviour.

Progressions

- If you want a specific position, such as a down, you can jackpot your dog to capture such a behaviour if, at some stage, he naturally offers it on the bed/in the crate. Alternatively, you can cue and reward that position.

- Lengthen the time gap between rewards. If your dog gets off the bed at any point, quickly and calmly return him to position. Be consistent; he needs to stay there until your release cue.

- Increase the distance between you and the bed/crate.
- Gradually increase distractions while your dog is in position but maintain a high level of success.

Teach your dog that staying in place will be rewarded.

During a training session with a friend, I noticed my dog had released himself and was merrily trotting around my venue. I told him he was a cheeky little moose and to go back to his bed! My friend pointed out I had released him five minutes earlier –and promptly forgotten about it. Oops! At least my dog knew what he was doing.

ON-OFF CUES

Imagine someone starts telling you about a gooey chocolate pudding, sprinkled with chopped nuts and crushed meringue. Or a hot steak sandwich, sizzling in butter, topped with onions and slowly melting cheese. You are probably going to start thinking about food and feeling hungry. You may not have seen or tasted the food but, by association, those words have made you think about it.

You can make use of this concept in training by getting your dog's focus and attention as if it was at the flick of a switch. To do this, pair his favourite reward with a cue of your choice. For example, if your dog loves interactive tug games, every time you tug with him say: "get it, get it!" Next try saying the cue – his 'on' switch – and then getting out the tug. You should be able to see a change in his body language that shows he is starting to anticipate the fun game!

Introduce a different cue – an 'off' switch – to mark the finish of the focused time. For example, when you stop tugging and your dog has let go of the toy, say: "chill out now", and discourage further interaction. Let him be a dog – for example sniffing, lying down, self-grooming or just mooching around.

Going forward, use your switch 'on' cue to signal the start of a training exercise, and your switch 'off' cue to signal the finish.

VERBAL DISCRIMINATION

A couple of years down the line, your dog will be zooming his way around an agility course. Picture the scene – as he completes the last weave pole you're telling him to pick the dog walk rather than the tunnel that's underneath it... Discrimination challenges are an obvious example of where verbal cues are crucial to brilliant and successful agility.

Teaching your dog to distinguish words is massively useful – it helps him learn how to tell one word from another and helps him to identify, more distinctly, all of your individual verbal cues. Dogs tend to be naturally aware of subtle visual distinctions but verbal distinctions, typically, take a bit more practice.

This is what to do:

Choose two behaviours which your dog already knows well, such as sit and down.

- Work on some sit behaviours. Graduate towards getting the behaviour with only your word to cue it, without any physical gestures or other visual cues. Be super aware of your body language so you don't give any hints, such as arm position, where you are looking, etc. Reward each sit behaviour.

- In another session, work on some down behaviours. Again, focus on getting the behaviour solely on a word cue. Keep your body neutral and identical to how it was when you asked for the sit.

- Keep working on this over a few sessions, concentrating on one behaviour – sit, for example – per session. Be aware of the pitch, and tone, of your voice when you give your verbal cues as your dog will be attuned to this.

- Next, start to vary your verbal cues, sometimes asking for a sit and sometimes for a down. Remember to rely on your words alone and avoid giving information with your body.

Don't be surprised or disappointed if it takes some time to crack this exercise. It's harder than it sounds!

Progressions

If your dog has mastered the exercise outlined above, you can try pushing it to another level:

- Work a third cue so that your dog is distinguishing between a greater number of words. Add in another, and so on. Remember to keep the success rate high.

- Another challenging variation is to deliberately use body language. This is unhelpful, as you ask with your words for a behaviour. For example, if you have your hands up near your face, can your dog still do a down on your verbal cue? Many dogs will initially offer a sit when the reward is in a higher position. This challenge mimics a typical agility scenario where you might be running towards a tunnel entrance but shouting "weave, weave," as you ask your dog to find the weave entry which lies just beyond the tunnel mouth.

STOP!

When you and your dog are negotiating an agility course, there will be times when your dog will need to slow down at the very moment your movement is showing the opposite. For example, you cue a weave entry and then race to do a blind cross at the weave exit. Or your dog approaches a tight spacing between two jumps while you run forward to cue the off end of the tunnel which follows.

The stop game teaches your dog how to separate his movement from what you are doing, in preparation for these challenges. Play the verbal discrimination game (see page 55) before attempting this.

This is what to do:

Your dog needs to give the position you cue regardless of what you are doing.

- Pick the position that your dog is most adept at offering from sit, stand and down. Stand by his side, and ask for the chosen behaviour a few times. Reward and release after each go. (If you have always cued this behaviour facing your dog, it may take a few sessions for him to get used to offering it by your side).

- Next, walk forward very slowly as you ask for the behaviour. The aim is for your dog to respond to the cue while you keep moving. Reward your dog when he is in the static position by returning to him, and then releasing.

- As you continue rehearsing this exercise, work towards moving more quickly while your dog stops and performs the position.

Progressions

- Do this exercise as you run.

- If you are giving both a visual and verbal cue when you ask for the position, try just using one or the other.

- Incorporate the verbal discrimination game into this exercise by varying which position you ask for.

Chapter Four

AGILITY SKILL SET

"A champion is someone who doesn't settle for that day's practice, that day's competition, that day's performance. They are always striving to be better."

Briana Scurry

Agility courses are simply sequences of skills. Examples of skills include sending to a tunnel, independence in the weaves and distance push rounds.

The better your dog's skills, the easier your job as a handler – you simply let your dog know which skill you require and when. Skills also make your dog faster. For instance, a dog who knows he is heading towards a pull through slice can decide exactly how many strides to take on the approach.

Honing your skills will make it easier for you and your dog to be clear and fast across multiple sequences.

When it comes to telling your dog which skill you need him to perform, you can use verbal cues (what you say) and visual cues (what you do) to initiate them. For example, if you want to send your dog around the backside of a jump, you might say "out" and raise your arm.

In terms of your visual cues, it's generally best to cue skills with your upper body more than your lower body. Agility courses these days are fast – dogs commonly achieve course times of upwards of 5-6 metres (16-20ft) per second. Not needing your lower body to give

HANDLING SKILLS

Each course demands a range of skills depending on the level at which you are competing. In this course, designed by Paul Hinchley, there is scope for the following skills:

- Push rounds: At jumps 2, 4 and 11.

- Discrimination: At 9 where it is tunnel not dog walk.

- Send to tunnel: At 10, 18, 19.

- Independent weaves: At 14

- Pull through slice: At jumps 2 or 4.

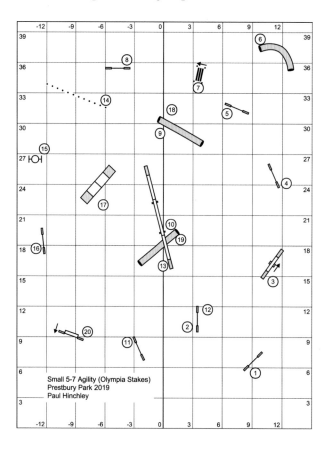

Small 5-7 Agility (Olympia Stakes)
Prestbury Park 2019
Paul Hinchley

information to your dog means you can concentrate on using your feet to move around the course efficiently. During skill training, it is therefore useful to proof your dog to ignore your feet.

HOW TO APPROACH SKILL TRAINING

Broadly speaking, skill training is a process of:

- Generating a behaviour (for example by shaping or luring).
- Pairing the behaviour with a cue that will eventually initiate the behaviour.
- Proofing the behaviour across multiple contexts.

When you introduce a new concept to your dog – whether that is a pull through, 2on-2off, or whatever other behaviour you are setting out to train – think of your first session as exposure to the task. Your sole aim is to introduce the behaviour to your dog. Do not expect understanding or mastery, and do not expect him to achieve a certain stage by the end of the session. When you have shown him the behaviour you want, stop right there, and don't go any further until your next session, on another day.

In fact, a lot will be absorbed in the passive, in-between time that separates your sessions. You may finish a session thinking your dog has not grasped a concept, only to find that at the start of the next session – fresh and having had time to assimilate your information – he is performing it well.

Once behaviours are becoming strong, you can structure a session by establishing the behaviour you want and then repeating it, raising the difficulty level. Imagine you are refining a weave entry. You might practise it first from close by the weaves, and then repeat it, but increase distance and speed to the approach.

Remember that agility is physically demanding on your dog. Training a weave entry, and increasing the degree of difficulty, is a bit like starting with press-ups from your knees and then going into a series of full press-ups. Your dog may gain a better mental understanding of the behaviour as the session progresses, but it will become harder and harder for his body to carry out that behaviour. Be aware of both the physical and mental effort involved in skill training.

TEACHING COMMITMENT

Imagine you are handling a sequence and you cue the tunnel. Your dog should now go and do the tunnel even if, before he's entered it, you run off in the opposite direction. This is the concept of commitment, and here is how it works:

- You cue a skill. For example, you say "tunnel" and push your arm towards the tunnel entry.

- Your dog mentally commits to the behaviour. He understands your cue and makes up his mind to carry it out. You see him look at the tunnel and begin to drive towards it.

- You leave, and your dog is aware of you leaving.

- Your dog does the behaviour, i.e. he goes into the tunnel and emerges at the other end.

Your dog will learn the commitment point you practise. For example, if you always wait until he has taken off for a jump before you turn and leave, you will always need to handle him that way. If he gets used to you leaving when he is still on the way to the jump, he will learn an earlier commitment point.

The earlier your dog's commitment point, the more efficiently you will be able to move around a course. The most competitive agility partnerships tend to be ones in which the dog is accustomed to the handler leaving very soon after a skill is cued.

The aim is for your dog to complete the task you have asked for, regardless of where you are on the course.

TIPS FOR SKILLS TRAINING

- Many skills are massively physically demanding. Your dog needs to be well developed and fit enough before you start the skill.

- Skills are mentally demanding. Be kind and patient and make sure you have covered plenty of life skills before beginning agility training (see Chapter Four).

- Be aware of how many repetitions you do during a session, and make increases incremental. Remember, agility is a sport that demands short and intense bursts, with plenty of rest in between.

- Gradually increase the amount of body movement you are showing while your dog performs any new skill – that movement can be distracting.

- When working on improving your dog's commitment, there will be times where he hesitates and opts to come with you rather than commit to the obstacle. That's normal. It often helps if you immediately pause and look back to where you would like him to be. If he then offers the behaviour you want after a moment or two, give him a small reward for having the right idea.

- Be aware of your dog's physique and the quality of his movement. You want your dog to learn fast, sustainable behaviours. Your focus should not be on *whether* your dog is doing an exercise but on *how* he is doing it. Get into the habit of observing him closely so you can evaluate how he is using his body.

- If you find it hard to assess your dog, video him in slow motion and then play it back for close analysis. It can also be helpful to watch some of the top agility dogs online and compare the way these dogs use their bodies to your own dog's behaviour. Dogs will resolve manoeuvres in different ways, dependent on their conformation, flexibility, eyesight, stride length, and the way they are taught, but the more you observe the better your eye will become.

- Remember to use your dog's 'on' and 'off' switches during training sessions (see page 54). When you need to initiate a break – to regroup, to get more treats, etc. – use your 'off' cue and allow him to mooch around, or send him to his bed or crate so he can rest and relax for a period. When it's time to start work, prompt him with your 'on' cue that tells him it's time to get started.

- When you are teaching a new skill, start work in a low arousal environment and use a reward which makes your dog interested, rather than over-excited or bored. Raise excitement levels gradually.

- Introduce verbal and visual cues by association. Your dog should have a 95 per cent chance of succeeding at the behaviour you are associating with the cue.

- Be precise with your cues so that you open up a clear channel of communication with your dog. For example, "round" is a different cue from "go round"; "weave" is different to "go weavers".

- When transferring from single obstacle skill work to longer sequences of skills, periodically reward mid-sequence to mark your dog's brilliance.

- Keep your dog's rate of success high and treat his failures as fun and normal.

There are four categories of skill training: general agility skills, jump and tunnel skills, contact skills and weave skills, which are covered in the following chapters.

Chapter Five

GENERAL AGILITY SKILLS

"The most important thing is to trust in the dog's skills!"
Sari Mikkila

When you teach general agility skills, you are laying the foundations of an invisible link – a connection – between you and your dog. These are fundamental handler-dog skills, which will encourage your dog to value and respond to your cues, even when speed and obstacles are later added into the mix.

FOLLOW MY BODY

When you are negotiating an agility course, your dog will often need to watch your body language carefully so that he can follow your directions.

Why?

If your body indicates a minor change of direction, it could be the difference between your dog going into an off-course tunnel, or driving towards the correct obstacle. In this exercise your dog learns the value in reading your movement and direction of travel.

How?

- Hold a reward in the hand closest to your dog, and move away from him. Encourage him to run to your hand and get the reward.

- Now try some circles. Keep turning on a loose circle, ensuring your dog stays close to you – almost as if he is on a lead. Encourage him to follow the hand with the reward by periodically rewarding him from it.

- Vary the size of the circle, encouraging your dog to mimic your changes in movement. Reward periodically.

- Enlist a helper to restrain your dog, or ask him to wait. Move away and then release him. As he gets near you, start to turn on a circle, encouraging him to come directly to your side rather than drifting out on the turn. Reward periodically, close to your side.

- Vary the distance between you and your dog before you release him. Increasing speed makes the exercise more of a challenge!

FRONT CROSS AND BLIND CROSS

When you are ahead of your dog on a course and do a front cross or a blind cross, your dog needs to understand that this means he must switch sides.

The difference between a front and a blind cross is the direction the handler is facing. For a front cross, you get ahead of your dog and face him as you ask him to change sides. For a blind, you are still ahead of your dog, but this time you face away from him as you do the exchange.

Why?

When you start to sequence obstacles with your dog, you will be using front crosses and blind crosses. As well as responding to your handling, your dog will also need to think about how to complete the obstacles correctly. It makes sense to teach crosses to your dog first as a groundwork exercise.

How?

- Enlist a helper to restrain your dog, or ask him to wait.

- Move ahead of him, making sure he can see his reward, which should be held in your right hand.

- Look back at your dog over your right shoulder and release him. Then make a front cross or a blind cross as he drives towards you. As you do so, exchange your reward so your dog can see it in your left hand. When your dog arrives by your left side, reward him from your left hand.

- Repeat on the opposite side.

Progressions

- Instead of using the reward to help your dog understand the change of side, hide it in a pocket until he's completed the behaviour and then reward him.

Once your dog has learnt to do tunnels (see page 75), position a tunnel on your right side. Well before he reaches the tunnel, make a cross and ask him to come to your left side, ignoring the beckoning tunnel entry.

- Mix up your handling so, occasionally, you don't make a cross. This will stop your dog anticipating that there will always be a change of side.

- Combine two crosses. For example, release your dog and do a blind, then do another blind. Reward once both are complete.

- Incorporate some obstacles – your dog won't be doing the obstacles, they are there as distractions. .

For more information on handling fronts and blinds, see page 155.

REAR CROSS

When you do a rear cross you turn your dog away from you and pass your dog from one side of you to the other. Rear crosses are also known as cross behinds. Sub-categories of rear cross are sometimes called lap turns, whisky turns or scoops – but they are all effectively rear crosses.

For more information on rear crossing, see page 156.

Why?

When you are sequencing obstacles, your dog will, typically, run in such a way that he is balanced to turn inward towards you. If you want him to turn away from you, you need to cue a rear cross. Just as with the front and the blind cross, your dog needs to respond to your handling as well as completing the obstacle correctly. It therefore makes sense to start teaching rear crosses as a groundwork exercise.

How?

- Before starting, decide on the visual cue you are going to use for a rear cross. Will you cue it with your on-arm (the one nearest your dog)? Or will you cue it with your off-arm (the one furthest from your dog)? The example used here uses the off arm.

- Start by practising the mechanics of this exercise on your own before trying it with your dog.

- Hold a reward in the hand you want your dog to follow.

- Bring your dog close to your right side. He should be almost touching you, and facing the same direction as you.

Position your reward hand close to your dog's nose. Then make an abrupt, sharp semi-circle with that hand. The semi-circle begins at your dog's nose and turns away from you. When your dog follows your hand and smoothly turns away from you, reward him in the position marked, Rwd.

Progressions

- Work on the exercise without the reward in your hand. Hide it in a pocket, but continue to reward after your dog has turned.

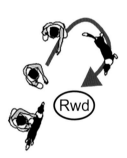

Add in some movement with your lower body. At first, use your lower body to help describe the turn you want your dog to make.

Now try keeping your lower body on a slow, continuous, straight line, and use your upper body to cue the rear cross as before – with your hand starting close to your dog's nose and making an abrupt, sharp semi-circle away from you. This is more complex, but very useful, as it explains to your dog how to do a rear cross without support from your feet.

Chapter Six

JUMP AND TUNNEL SKILLS

"With each stride a dog is making a decision."

Susan Salo

Jumps make up the majority of obstacles on agility courses so they are well worth the investment in training time. Work through the skills described here and you will be prepared to tackle complex jump and tunnel courses at speed.

These skills can be taught as tiny exercises, comprising one or two obstacles in your garden or training area. Once the skills are well understood and proofed, they can gradually be transferred to longer sequences.

TRAINING TIPS

- Initially use very low height jumps. Raise the height as the behaviour becomes well understood both mentally and physically.

- Lightweight poles are preferable.

- Where possible, train on wings and poles which replicate those you anticipate facing in competition. For example, some organisations use 1.5 metre (5ft) poles while others use 1.2 metres (4ft) as standard.

- Unless your canine health professional advises otherwise, balance all work so that 50 per cent of the time you are working on your dog's right side and 50 per cent of the time on his left. Your dog should be doing a roughly equal split of left and right turns.

- Use well-secured tunnels with decent interior grip. Avoid making the tunnel curve too acute.

- Be aware that there is better visibility inside a light-coloured tunnel than a darker one.

JUMP FOCUS

Teach your dog to focus on the jump in front of him while he is waiting to be released.

Why?

This behaviour is incredibly useful on a start-line. It allows the handler to be at a distance from the dog while the dog still looks at, and drives towards, the first obstacle. It can also be useful to get forward focus after stop contacts, for example, at the end of a seesaw.

By learning to look at the obstacle rather than the handler, the dog is more likely to jump it well. He will have had an opportunity to register his distance from the jump and its height. This exercise also helps your dog learn to see your handling as a sort of necessary distraction, which doesn't interfere with his own jumping style.

How?

Before working on this behaviour, make sure you have trained a solid wait (see page 50) and taught your dog to drive to a static and live reward (see page 44).

- Put your dog in a wait position facing a jump.
- Walk to the far side of the jump, and place your reward (a toy, for example) on the ground.
- Then walk back to a position beside or behind your dog (not in front of him).

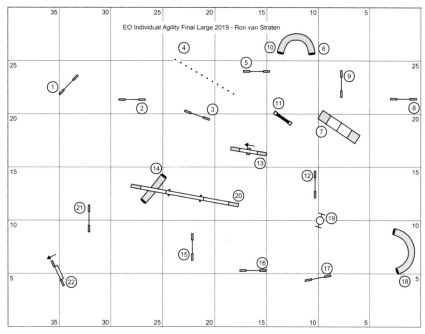

EO Individual Agility Final Large 2019 - Ron van Straten

Course designer: Ron van Straten

This course from the European Open finals, illustrates why forward focus at the first obstacle is an advantage. The handler can start somewhere near obstacles two to three, rather than supporting the line to the first jump.

- Wait until he looks forward at his reward, rather than looking at you. Release him to get his reward when he does so.

- Repeat this game, and start to increase the time that your dog looks at his reward before being released to clear the jump and get his reward. For example, he might be looking at the reward for two, four, and then six seconds before you release him.

- Vary your position. For example, you could be a few metres away to one side of him, behind him or in front of him.

- Vary where you position your dog in relationship to the jump. Try a range of angles and distances.

- Vary your movement. You might be moving forward, moving away to one side, or static.
- You now need to reduce the visibility of the reward to help your dog transition from reward-focus to obstacle-focus. There are a couple of ways to achieve this seamlessly:
  - Place a small reward, such as a cube of cheese, on the far side of the jump so that your dog can't gauge for sure whether it's there. After a few repetitions where your dog has discovered the cheese, walk out and pretend to put the cheese on the ground, as before. Instead, keep the cheese in your pocket, and throw it in after your dog has cleared the jump.
  - Alternatively, you can hide a toy reward in long grass, for example, and then play the game a couple of times. This way your dog learns that the toy is probably out there, even if he can't see it. Next, pretend to position the toy, as before, but keep it in your pocket. Throw in the reward after your dog has cleared the jump.
- Once your dog is no longer relying on a visible reward, keep playing the game but continue to wait until he is looking forward before releasing him. After he drives forward and clears the obstacle, toss in your reward.

Progressions

- Experiment by using different obstacles, such as the long jump.
- Continue to vary your movement and position.
- Introduce a cue to initiate this behaviour, for example "look." Alternatively, it can be a behaviour that you always expect and often reward in specific contexts – for example on the start-line – without using a specific cue to trigger the behaviour.
- Going forward, remember this behaviour. Anytime your dog is static in position before an obstacle, look for him to focus on that obstacle before you release.

The aim is for the dog to focus on the obstacle ahead.

TUNNEL DRIVE

This involves teaching your dog to power to, and through, a tunnel.

Why?

Send to tunnel is a common on-course skill. It might sound easy but there are lots of things that can make it harder, depending on the tunnel's position in the sequence. You might need your dog to commit to the tunnel from a distance, the dog might see the tunnel from an unusual angle, or it might be on the far side of another obstacle such as the dog-walk.

How?

- Start training with a really short tunnel, approximately 1-2 metres, (3-6ft), in length.

- You can shape the behaviour or lure it.

- If you are shaping, wait for your dog to offer successive behaviours of looking at the tunnel, moving towards it, going through it.

- If you are luring, place your reward two-thirds of the way through the tunnel, or just on the far side. The best plan is hold your dog by his harness and help him see the reward through the tunnel. Let go of him when you feel him pull forward in the right direction.

Help your dog to focus on his toy, placed at the far side of the tunnel.

Progressions

- Vary the length of the tunnel.

- Add your cues for your dog to do a tunnel.

- Gradually add a curve to the tunnel. Generally, position yourself on the inside of the curve. You can also try being on the outside, especially when the curve is gentle.

- Vary the angle of the tunnel entry in relation to your dog.

- Vary the distance between the tunnel and your dog's start position.

- Leave earlier as your dog drives to the tunnel. Play around with leaving in different directions.

- Vary the tunnel's position. It might be near other obstacles, for example, safely secured under (and not touching) the dog-walk.

- Add in crosses. For example, you could front or blind cross just before or just after the tunnel. Alternatively, you could turn your dog away from you to find the tunnel entry on a rear cross.

Test your dog's tunnel drive by varying his angle to, and distance from the tunnel entry.

Photo: Matt Bowen for www.winclinic.co.uk

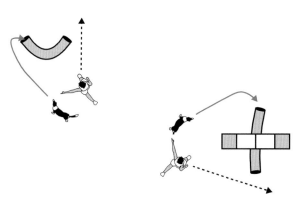

Here are a few examples of some trickier tunnel sends to try.

STRAIGHT LINE WORK

Jumps make up the majority of obstacles on most courses. This exercise helps teach your dog to jump effectively and efficiently, and how to drive down a line of jumps. He will grow in confidence, and you will be building the value he has in driving forward ahead of you.

Why?

This exercise teaches your dog to read a jump using the jump pole to gauge the height, and the distance to the jump. It helps him learn not to be distracted by unhelpful factors such as the wing feet. Even if you have an experienced dog, this is a great exercise to include in your training programme from time to time.

How?

Before doing this exercise, it's helpful if your dog has been introduced to cavaletti (see 79). To set up the jump exercise, you will need jump poles and something on which they can be positioned. Avoid using a jump wing or anything that is bulky. Use something small that allows the pole to easily be displaced in either direction, such as football training cones. To begin with, the pole should be very low to the ground.

- Position the pole on your low prop.
- Place your reward on the ground, at some distance beyond the pole.
- Preferably incorporate your forward focus exercise (see page 44) and wait for this behaviour before proceeding.
- Allow your dog to drive over the pole to get his reward.
- Repeat the exercise in both directions until your dog appears confident and competent.

What to watch for:

- The mid-point of your dog's jump arc should be nicely centred over the pole.

- Your dog should smoothly transition from striding over the ground to striding over the pole. This should happen without any excessive adjustment.

INTRODUCING CAVALETTI

A basic cavaletti grid is a straight line of around four poles arranged in a ladder formation. You can use jump poles positioned just off the floor on low cones. The poles should easily dislodge from the cones if your dog touches them.

- Hold your dog on a lead clipped to his harness and encourage him to walk through the poles. You want him to find a steady four-beat walk gait.

- Adjust the poles to suit your dog's stride length – each foot should fall roughly halfway between each pole.

- Watch for your dog maintaining an even rhythm and comfortably avoiding making contact with the poles.

Keep a loose lead and allow the dog to find his own rhythm.

Progressions

- Increase and then vary the number of poles-on-props, up to around five.

- Introduce a 'send-down-a-line-of-jumps' cue to this behaviour, such as "go on, go on!", towards the finish of a course when your dog has a straight run of a couple of jumps to finish.

- Vary the angle of the poles, by propping one side up a little higher than the other, or by making one side a little further forward than the other.

- Vary the height of the poles.

- Vary your position. You could be ahead of your dog, beside him or behind him.

- Vary your movement. You might be running or accelerating or just walking.

- Add some jump wings, as distractions. Initially, scatter a few wings around your pole set-up. Then increase the number of wings and put them in jump-like formation, with two wings facing each other. Your dog should continue with the exercise, ignoring the wings.

- You can incorporate spreads into this set-up. To create a spread, prop the poles on to almost-invisible supports in a rising or parallel formation. Wings should only be used as distractions.

WING WRAP

This skill involves your dog turning neatly around the wing of a jump. There is a balance to be struck between tightness and speed, which is both dog and scenario dependent.

GRIDWORK

Your dog's jumping ability will also improve with gridwork exercises. During gridwork, you use specific formations of jumps to grow your dog's confidence, and experience, and to encourage a capable jump style.

There are many resources available to help you, both online and in the form of books and dvds such as those by Susan Salo.

The optimal form is usually for the dog to be slightly loose on the approach, allowing him to rotate his body pre take-off. He will then be ready to land and power off in the new direction.

Why?

There will be multiple occasions on course where your dog needs to collect and turn abruptly around a jump wing. As he does so, you could be doing one of a number of possible moves, such as a front or blind cross, a ketschker or pivot (see Chapter 10: Handling).

How?

- First decide on your verbal cue. Some handlers use different cues for a wing wrap to the left or right; other handlers use a single cue for a wing wrap, regardless of the direction. Think of the cue as meaning: drive to the obstacle, wrap around the wing and drive back towards me. Avoid adding extra verbals to your cue. For example, if your cue is "check check", avoid "go check check".

If your dog has strong commitment you can leave him to perform the move – in this case a ketschker – while you move off to the next part of the course.

Photo: Matt Bowen for www.winclinic.co.uk

- Decide on your visual cue. Most handlers use arm signals to support their wing wrap cues. These may differ depending on the handling move, so a ketschker may look slightly different to a pivot wrap.

Begin your wing wrap training by shaping your dog to turn towards you around an obstacle on the flat. This could be a cone, a barrel, a bin, or a jump wing. You may find it easier to reward with food. There is no need to encourage speed at first. Build in speed as your dog learns how to balance his body through the turn. Use your reward position to encourage him to turn tightly.

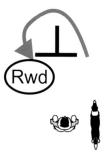

- If your dog starts on your left, he will be turning right around the wing. If he starts on your right, he will be turning left.

Observe your dog's form and how he is using his body to complete the behaviour. It takes time, strength and flexibility for him to master his technique. Be alert to your dog tiring during wrap games. Quality should be your focus, not quantity.

Progressions

- Transfer the behaviour to a single jump wing (if you haven't already used one).

- Add your verbal and visual cues so that your dog starts to learn them by association.

- Do some multi-wraps. As your dog receives his reward, cue a second wrap immediately and reward again. Once your dog can do this, try a series of two wraps which are not broken up by a reward.

- Transfer the behaviour to an entire jump with a very low pole.

- Practise initiating the behaviour solely on a verbal cue (showing no movement at all).

- Practise initiating the behaviour solely on a visual (saying nothing).

- Alternate the handling move as your dog turns around the wing. For example, you might do a pivot, a ketshcker, a front cross and so on.

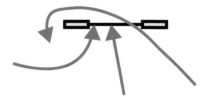

Vary the angle of approach to the jump – especially working sharp angles.

- Gradually increase the distance from which you cue the jump to two metres (6ft), five metres (16ft), seven metres (22ft) and 10 metres (33ft). Cue the wrap without showing any movement towards the jump.

- As your dog drives towards the wing wrap, leave and move away from the jump. For example, as he heads towards the jump begin a pivot, turning away swiftly as you do so. By the time he has completed the wrap you want to be some distance away. This is a great exercise to improve your dog's wing wrap commitment. Gradually push yourself to leave earlier – immediately after you have given the cue to do a wrap. Vary your speed and vary the direction in which you leave. Keep rewarding your dog as soon as he has wrapped the wing.

- Incorporate some trap obstacles nearby. For example, position a tunnel near to the wing and then to the landing side of the jump, which is irrelevant to the exercise. Keep it at a distance that will still allow your dog to succeed. You can bring it closer as his understanding grows.

The dog must commit to the wing wrap, and ignore the draw of the tunnel.

REAR CROSS WRAP

Your dog may need to wrap around a wing by turning away from you. This is a rear cross wing wrap. If you do not turn your feet in the same direction as your dog is going, you are doing a type of rear cross which is sometimes called a lap turn or a scoop.

Why?

When you are sequencing obstacles, there may be times when it is more efficient to keep your dog on your outside and turn him away from you.

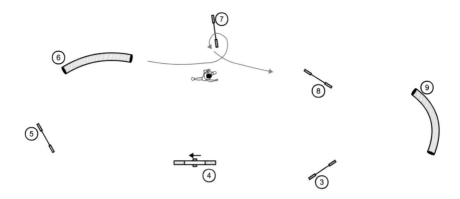

In this sequence, it may be quicker to get away if you keep your dog on your left going into obstacle 7, rather than transitioning him to your right, and then needing to get him back to your left side.

How?

- Remind yourself of your visual rear cross cue (see page 69). Decide whether you want to have a specific verbal rear cross wing wrap cue, or just use the cue you use for ordinary turn-towards-you wraps. Think about what you will do, visually, for this move – it's probably going to be similar to what you did when you practised the rear cross groundwork.

- Revisit the rear cross exercise (see pages 69-70).

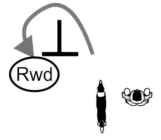

Now, position a jump wing close to your dog. When you ask your dog to turn away from you, look for him to turn around the wing. Initially, you can turn your feet with your dog as he goes around the wing. Reward as illustrated, so that his reward is available to him as he completes his turn around the wing.

- Next, try doing some wraps without turning your feet.

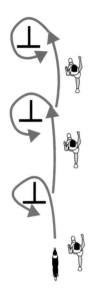

Try sequencing several wings together. The more you travel as your dog commits to each wing, the more difficult it is. Begin by rewarding after each wing.

Progressions

- Transfer the behaviour to a jump with a very low pole.
- Vary the angle of approach to the jump.
- Increase the distance between your starting point and the jump to two metres (6ft), five metres (16ft), seven metres (22ft) and 10 metres (33ft).
- As your dog drives towards the rear cross wrap, leave and move away from it. Vary the direction in which you leave. Gradually push yourself to leave earlier and with more speed.

PULL THROUGH SLICE

When you ask your dog for a pull through, you are asking him to commit to the side of the obstacle that you on, or travelling towards.

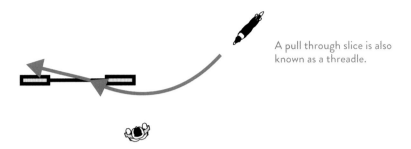

A pull through slice is also known as a threadle.

Why?

The requirement to make an S shape on a jump, during a sequence, is a challenge frequently set by judges.

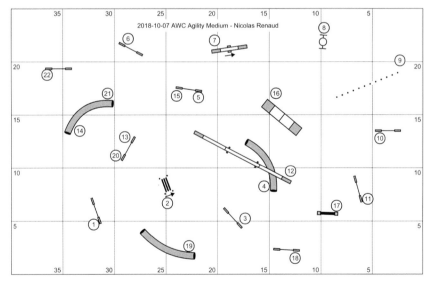

Course designer: Nicolas Renaud

Look at jump 13 on this course. If you kept the dog-walk on your left, jump 13 could be handled as a pull through slice.

How?

- Before beginning, think about your words and signals. You need a clear, distinct verbal cue. In terms of a visual cue, some handlers use their on-arm (nearest the dog) pulled back behind them; others use their off-arm (furthest from the dog), with the hand as a fist in a grabbing motion.

Upper body cues for a pull through slice using the on-arm (pictured left), and bringing the off-arm into play (pictured right).

- Initially, break the behaviour into two parts. This makes it more manageable for your dog both physically and mentally. The first part teaches your dog to come to your side, the second part encourages him to commit to the jump on a slice.
- Start one metre (3ft) or so away from the jump and hold some treats in the hand that will be cueing the move. Encourage your dog to come to your hand and reward.

- Continue to reward, keeping him at your side, until you are very close to the jump. Now encourage him to go over the pole and drop a treat on the ground once he has done so (see below).

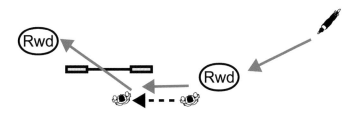

Progress towards starting closer to the jump. Give a single reward at your side before your dog does the jump, and then give him a second reward.

- Cut out the reward given at your side, and only reward after your dog has done the jump. Look for him to start assuming he is to go over the jump without needing any indication or help from you.

- Add your cue word. The cue word means: come-to-my-side-of-the-obstacle-and-commit-to-the-obstacle.

With clear visual signals for a pull through slice, the dog is able to take the most economic line.

Progressions

- Vary your movement. Do some with your feet totally still, and do some where you move quite a lot.

- Do some where you are closer to the jump, and some where you are further away.

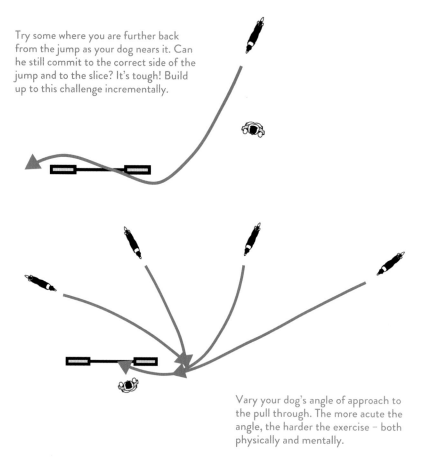

Try some where you are further back from the jump as your dog nears it. Can he still commit to the correct side of the jump and to the slice? It's tough! Build up to this challenge incrementally.

Vary your dog's angle of approach to the pull through. The more acute the angle, the harder the exercise – both physically and mentally.

- Try some multiple pull throughs, using two or three separate jumps.

PULL THROUGH WRAPS

Pull through wraps are similar to pull through slices as your dog still commits to the side of the jump that you are on, or travelling towards.

Rather than then slicing over the jump, he turns away from you and wraps around the inside wing of the jump.

Why?

This move is handy when it's the fastest route on the jump, and it's impossible, or slower, for you to get to the other side of your dog. Although this is a fairly technical move, it is very useful once mastered.

How?

- Make sure that you have practised some rear crossing with your dog before starting this move (see page 69).

- Decide on the word and signal you will use to cue this behaviour. They will need to be different to your pull through slice cues.

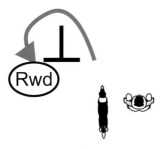

Begin working with a single wing. Your dog needs to be on your off-side. If he is on your right, he will be turning right around the wing. If he is on your left, he will be turning left. Stand very close to the wing, with your dog beside you, making sure you are completely still. Using your body language, encourage your dog to do a rear cross around the wing. Reward him in position, just after he turns around the wing.

91

- Repeat and, as you do so, focus on using only upper body visual signals to get your dog to do the behaviour. Avoid turning your feet.

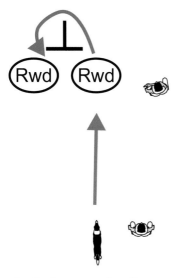

Next, try starting a little further away from the wing and then continue to travel forward as your dog does the rear cross wrap (see 84). If you find your dog moves away from you as you approach the wing, you may want to give two rewards, as shown by the positions marked – one by your side delivered just before the wing, and the second after he has turned around the wing.

- Gradually increase the distance between your starting point and the wing.

- As your dog's confidence and success grows, add the verbal and visual cues you have chosen to use for a pull through wrap.

- Increase your forward movement during the behaviour. This helps proof your dog to ignore your feet.

- Transition from working on a single wing to working with an entire jump. If your dog starts to slice, rather than wrap, be prepared to go back to using a single wing.

Progressions

- Continue to vary the distance from your starting point and the jump.

- Vary your speed.

Your dog needs to be familiar with rear crossing before working on a pull through wrap.

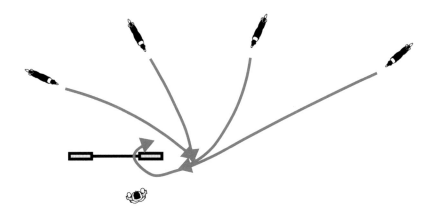

Play around with the angle of approach that you, and your dog, take into the behaviour.

- Once your dog is awesome at this behaviour, test his understanding by alternating between asking for a pull through slice and a pull through wrap.

SERPS AND GERMANS

During a serp (or serpentine) you are ahead of your dog as he comes towards you, and then goes away from you again. Even though the move involves your dog making slight changes of direction, he stays on the same side of you throughout. *For information on handling serps, see page 159.*

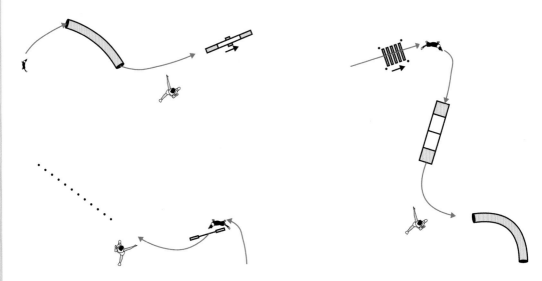

A serp is also any line on a course which resembles that type of S-line. Here are a three examples of serp lines. Note that during a serp the dog always stays on the same side of the handler.

Why?

Training a serp allows you to tackle this element in sequences. It is also the key to training great germans. A german is where, immediately after a serp element, the handler adds in a blind. A german is a serp-blind, also known as a collection-blind. *For information on handling germans, see page 160.*

How?

The aim is to teach your dog to carry out a serp based on your arm cue and your visual contact over one shoulder. Your dog should ignore your feet, allowing you to move off rather than needing to slow down or wait for him.

Most handlers do not have a verbal cue specifically for a serp, although other cues may be used if the serp incorporates specific movement patterns. For example, it may be relevant to use a wing wrap cue if your dog needs to turn tightly around a wing as he performs the serp.

Teaching your dog to have brilliant serp commitment in response to your arm cue is the key both to great serps and great germans.

- First, rehearse what you are going to do. Position your feet in the direction in which you are going. Avoid rotating your feet unnecessarily – you want your dog to learn to commit to the serp without any help from your feet.

- Practise your arm cue. Some handlers use a single on-arm for a serp cue, and others use both arms together. In either case, imagine you are opening a door behind you with your arm(s).

- Set your dog up in front of a single jump and position yourself on the far side of it. Release him and use the arm signal you want him to learn as his serp cue. As you are doing this, look over your shoulder at the direction in which he should commit.

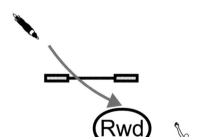

Throw the reward back to your dog as he drives over the jump, making sure it falls near his landing spot. Don't reward from your hand; you want to build value in the dog committing to the obstacle which is just behind you, not driving with you.

Progressions

- Add a little movement of your feet – from slow to fast.
- Vary your distance from the jump.

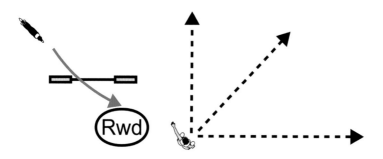

Vary your line of travel as the dog commits to the jump. You could be moving away in a diagonal direction, or crossing the plane of the jump.

- Throw the reward to your dog a bit later, so there is no likelihood of luring the behaviour; you are rewarding him after he has already decided to commit to the jump.

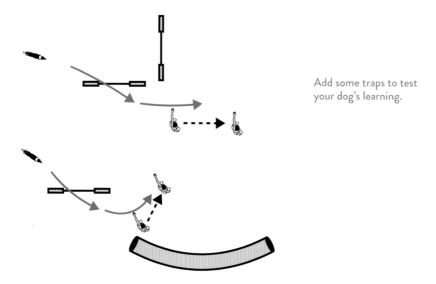

Add some traps to test your dog's learning.

GERMAN

A serp can be followed by a blind, turning it into a german. Here's an example of a sequence during which a german is useful.

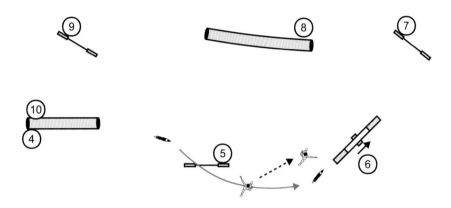

As a handler, you can choose to do the blind at any point. There will be lots of times when it is appropriate to do the switch as the dog does the obstacle (see above and below).

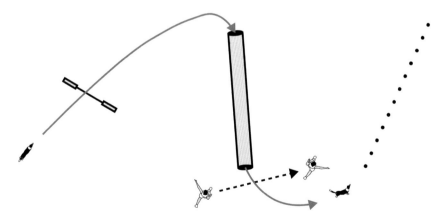

There will also be occasions when you want to transition from serp to blind at a different time. In this example doing the blind as your dog does the jump would increase the likelihood of him going in the off-course tunnel.

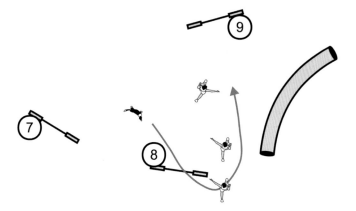

Instead, you would need to keep connection with your dog on your left side until he has committed to coming with you in the direction of jump 9. You would, therefore, hold him on the serp. To do this you would still run forward, but you would continue to look back over your left shoulder and keep your left arm extended. When your dog reached approximately one-third of the way between jumps 8 and 9, you would then switch to the blind, connecting with your dog over your right shoulder.

A serp cues collection and asks your dog to slow down. It tells him to stay on the same side of you. When you transition from cueing a serp to cueing a blind cross, you ask your dog to extend, accelerate and drive to the other side of you.

Experiment with your germans to understand how switching from your serp to your blind influences your dog's behaviour.

How?

- Repeat the first serp exercise (see page 95), but as your dog commits to the jump, make a blind and encourage him to finish on your new side.

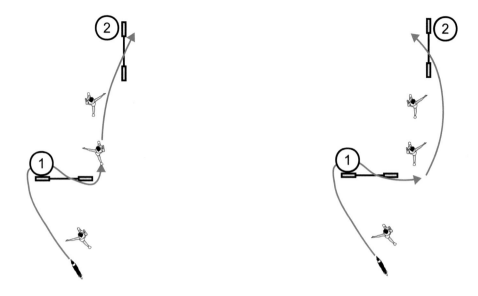

Try these two exercises so you can experiment with the timing of your blind. If you haven't explored push rounds with your dog yet, save these exercises until you have.

PUSH ROUNDS/BACKSIDES

When you ask for a push round, your dog is presented with the option of taking the incorrect front of the jump; instead he needs to respond to your cues by driving to, and then taking, the backside of the jump.

Why?

Push rounds are a common feature on courses, especially those at a higher level. With training that establishes a good understanding, your dog will able to go and do the behaviour independently. This means there is no need for you to go all the way to the jump wing with him, nor to wait until he's taken off for the backside before you move off.

How?

The most common visual cue for a push round is to use the on-arm to signal up and away from the body.

A distinct verbal cue is vital for your push round behaviour, so your dog never confuses it with any cue that tells that him to commit to the front of the jump. Common verbal cues are "back," "out" or "round". When cueing your push round, avoid preceding it with "go". A cue such as "go round", for example, is contradictory if you use "go" to cue the front of the jump.

Initially, avoid training push rounds at the same time as training wing wraps. Doing so can be confusing as they can seem similar from a dog's perspective. When training push rounds use a pole with your jump wing, or an entire jump, from the outset to help your dog differentiate them from wraps.

Shape your push round behaviour. Begin with you and your dog positioned very close to the side of the jump he should be pushing towards. Wait for him to commit to the backside of the jump, or at least move or look in the desired direction, before throwing your reward to land so that he gets it just as he comes back over the pole towards you.

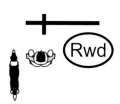

- Repeat until your dog is driving confidently around the backside of the jump each time.

- Introduce your verbal cue and then your visual cue. Continue to reward in roughly the same position, i.e. as he comes back over the pole towards you.

Progressions

- Increase the distance from your starting point to the jump, building up to around 10m.

- Vary the angle from which your dog is approaching the jump.

- Vary how much you are moving.

- Vary your own direction of travel.

- Once your dog is proficient at push rounds, it is useful to test and improve the behaviour by asking him, intermittently, to commit to the front of the jump instead of the backside.

A frequent challenge on courses is to ask the dog to commit to a push round and then perform a serp or a german. Rehearse these moves, making sure your dog continues to commit to the serp/german out of the push round, even when you are travelling forward and crossing the plane of the jump.

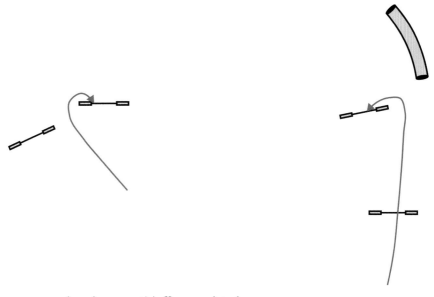

Introduce potential off-course obstacles near your push rounds, such as other jumps and tunnels.

VERBAL DISCRIMINATION

Your dog has to discriminate between the verbal cues you give him as you work your way around a course. For example, imagine your dog is getting ahead of you as he races towards a jump. Do you want him to push round the wing, or wrap it, which is the exact opposite? In this situation, your dog must be guided by your verbal cue. Once your dog learns to understand and distinguish one word cue from another, he will be an easier partner for you to handle, and his confidence will grow.

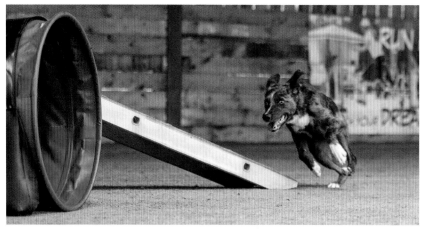

There are times when a dog needs to rely solely on a verbal cue to tell him which obstacle to take.

Why?

It's all very well training lots of different skills associated with different verbal cues, but if your dog can't differentiate them, what's the point? He needs to run at speed, deal with all the distractions of a competition environment, and still process and respond to what you are saying! This has to be taught. It's a tough skill as dogs are, by nature, much better attuned to your body language than to your words.

How?

Remember how we looked at verbal discrimination as a pre-agility skill (see page 55). Now it's time to take this learning to the equipment. You can work verbal discrimination on any pieces of equipment: contacts and tunnels, or weaves and tunnels, for example. Here, we will use jump skills:

- You can only teach discrimination when your dog understands how to do each behaviour purely on a verbal cue. To start, pick two jump skills, for example push rounds and wing wraps.

- Working on a single jump, ask for some push rounds. Now sit on the floor and give your verbal cue. This will stop you using your body to help your dog. Start asking for push rounds, solely on a verbal cue.

- After a break, do some wing wraps on the same jump. Again, progress to sitting on the floor, and give your verbal cue from there.

- If your dog is struggling to complete the required behaviours solely on verbal cues, keep practising until you, and your dog, have mastered each individual behaviour beautifully.

- Next make the break a bit shorter. Ask for two or three push rounds, on a verbal, with you seated. Pause. Remain seated, then ask for two or three wing wraps, on a verbal cue.

This is tough, so be patient. You are unlikely to crack it in a single session. You may find it helps if you prepare your dog by giving him the cue a few times before asking him to perform it.

Progressions

- Get rid of the break – go straight from one behaviour to the next.

- Continually vary which behaviour you are asking for so your dog can't pattern any kind of routine. Ask for a push round, then ask for a wing wrap, then another wing wrap, then a push round... and so on.

- Gradually add in a third cue. For example, once your dog can do a rear cross wing wrap on a unique verbal, bring this cue into the mix. Sometimes ask for a push round, sometimes a wing wrap and sometimes a rear cross wing wrap.

- Remember, you can play this exercise with any two or more of your verbal cues.

WHAT IS PATTERNING?

Dogs are smart. They learn patterns in your behaviour very quickly: that's what makes them easy to train. Repeat a behaviour with your dog a few times in a row and he may guess that your next cue will ask for the same behaviour.

Guessing, or patterning, is really useful sometimes. When you introduce your dog to a new skill, such as wrapping around a cone, and then want to increase its difficulty – by moving the cone further away, for example – the pattern your dog has learnt will help him work out what you want so he succeeds quickly.

Ultimately, in competition, your dog needs to respond to each individual cue, since you will want him to perform a range of different skills in quick succession. Discrimination games help to teach your dog to rely on your cues to figure out the behaviour you want.

Chapter Seven

WEAVE SKILLS

"It's not about the length of your legs. It's about trusting your dog, teaching him good commitment."

Silvia Trkman

There is a whole lot more to weaving than getting your dog to do 12 weaves in a row. Great weave skills free you up as a handler, allowing you to move around the course efficiently while your dog gets on with his job.

What exactly do I want?

Fabulous entries! Your dog needs to understand he must enter with the first pole on his left, regardless of his approach, and no matter what other equipment is close to that entry.

Sensational independence! Your dog needs to stay in those weaves until completion, ignoring distractions of nearby equipment and where you travel as he does them.

Speed! Your dog has to be able to use his body to collect as much as necessary to nail the entry. Once in, he needs to be physically fit and psychologically motivated to power through them as quickly as he can.

Weave Form

Watch carefully and you will notice that different dogs have different weaving patterns. There is no right or wrong; the best pattern is the one which allows your own individual dog to complete the obstacle accurately with maximum speed.

Some dogs use their hindlimbs and forelimbs together, driving through in a movement which goes from left hind and right hind to left fore and right fore, to left hind and right hind, and so on. Depending on which side of the weaves the dog is on, he will load his left and right limb differently on each consecutive step, based on which is on the inside and which is on the outside.

Two-stepping in the weaves – Shelley's preferred method.

Single footing in the weaves – Clyde's method of weaving.

Other dogs incorporate some single footing. For instance, you may spot a pattern whereby the dog combines left hind and right hind together, with a single alternate left fore, right fore, left fore, and so on.

Factors which influence the way a dog weaves include conformation, fitness and flexibility. There are also other external factors, such as the stability of the surface (the same dog may weave differently on loose sand to artificial grass), and how rigidly the weaves are fixed in position.

Injuries, and compensatory patterns, are commonly highlighted by the weaves. This could include loading a specific limb more than its symmetrical opposite, continually struggling with a particular entry despite training, slowing down, or appearing to dislike the weaves altogether. These are all red flags which may well signal injury or discomfort.

HOW TO TRAIN YOUR DOG TO WEAVE

Before embarking on weave training, bear in mind that the fitter, stronger and more body-aware your dog is, the easier it will be for him to develop a pattern, and the more efficient and fast that pattern is likely to be.

Competition-style closed weaves should not be attempted before your dog is physically well-developed. Weave work sessions should be kept short, and increases in weave training load should be incremental.

There are a number of methods you can use to teach your dog to weave, and there are benefits to each one. Some dogs are better suited to one method than another. You can also combine multiple methods.

TWO BY TWO

This is a method of teaching your dog to weave two poles at a time. So a two-pole behaviour is established, then a two-pole plus two-pole behaviour, and so on, until they are all combined and you have a 12-pole behaviour. Entry training is often incorporated from the outset.

This method is very useful for explaining the mental concept of weaves to your dog. Done well, your dog is likely to acquire a strong understanding of what is required by the weaves.

On the other hand, the two by two method does not present your dog with the incremental physical challenge that is provided with channel weaves, for example (see page 109).

V WEAVES

V weaves consist of poles which pivot from the base through 180 degrees. If you look along them, they make the shape of a letter V. At the outset, the poles can be set quite far apart, and then brought closer as your dog learns the required behaviour.

With V weaves, you can increase the physical difficulty of the task, while keeping the mental challenge fairly easy. Your dog can see his route through the weaves as they are wider higher up, even though lower down the gap is narrower, making the footwork more complex.

V weaves can encourage high head carriage, which tends to be an inefficient weave action. They can also result in the dog learning to push weave poles out of his path, which can cause problems when he transitions to fixed upright and inflexible poles. Depending on how they are used, the physical demand of V weaves is, typically, fairly challenging from the outset.

V weaves: The dog has a clear view through the weaves, even though the footwork is more complex.

CHANNEL WEAVES

With this method you begin with an open set of weaves with a big gap down the middle. Initially your dog is just running down a clear line with poles on either side of him. The poles are gradually brought closer until your dog is doing a weaving action. Ultimately, they are completely closed.

Channels can be very useful for training the physical action of a weave to your dog. The physical challenge is incrementally increased and, thus, your dog has the chance to adapt his physical behaviour as his strength and ability improves.

Care needs to be taken with the timing of when you close channel weaves. Too quickly, and your dog will not be able to understand, or perform, the challenge. Too slowly, and your dog may have become so accustomed to racing at speed that it takes him a while to understand he can't just run, but needs to use careful footwork.

Channel weaves: The degree of difficulty can be increased incrementally.

Some of the best channel weave sets enable the poles to be opened and closed individually rather than as a whole, meaning the difficulty level can be increased or decreased even more mindfully.

WEAVE GUIDES

Some handlers use weave guides in combination with one of the training methods, or on straight poles. These are flexible pieces of plastic which attach to alternate poles and ensure your dog navigates the correct route. To avoid going the correct route, he would need to crawl under, or leap over, the guides.

Weave guides can be functional for reducing failure because they make it a near certainty that your dog will complete the poles in the correct order. But avoid treating them as a quick fix when the dog is not physically primed for the task since the physical challenge is demanding from the outset.

TAKING YOUR 12-POLE WEAVE FORWARD

Vary the location of your weaves frequently at all stages during training. In terms of your strategy, think of keeping the weaves in the same place as useful for increasing your dog's weave speed and confidence, and varying the location as essential for teaching him to be weave-accurate in the longer term.

When your dog approaches the weaves in a competition setting, he will not be able to anticipate them. He doesn't know where they are in the ring, or when he will be asked to do them, so they always come as a surprise. The only warning is your cue. During training, give your dog the opportunity to learn how to cope both physically, and mentally, with this challenge. It is not something he will learn from rehearsing weaves in your garden, for example, where they have been fixed in the same position for the last three weeks.

When your dog is really weave-confident, train sequences in which he comes across the weaves in the same surprise way as he would in a trial. He should not have seen the weaves in exactly that place before so he will not be able to anticipate them, other than via your cue. This will help him learn to associate your early weave cue with performing the behaviour. It's essential he learns how to do this before weaving in competition.

Going from teaching a full 12-pole weave to putting your weaves into short sequences is a natural transition. However, you will find that success comes more readily if you have also prepared for the sequencing by working on your weave entries.

WEAVE ENTRIES

Aside from training your dog to complete 12 straight weave poles, there is also the business of teaching him how to find the weave entry, and being able to collect into that entry.

Initially, teaching your dog the entry, and training him to do 12 poles in order, are two distinct challenges. Thus, when working on nailing the 12-pole behaviour, keep the entry easy. When working on entry challenges, use just two or three poles (or if you are using more, reward after two or three poles) until he is really proficient. Ultimately, the two can be combined into one awesome behaviour.

For your dog to have a sensational weave entry, he needs to know how to do the behaviour on a mental level. In addition, he needs the physical ability to perform this complex behaviour at speed, and to perceive the value of doing so.

Agility people commonly talk about 'independent' weave entries. This can be a bit misleading. When handling your dog around a course, he is following every tiny movement and piece of information you provide. In competition, it is up to you to cue your dog (early enough for him to process and respond) via the words

Make sure you have a clear, distinctive verbal cue for the weave entry so your dog ignores off-course obstacles.

you say, and the things you do, in order to deploy the skill – i.e. to go and seek out the weave entry. Your dog should then understand the concept of finding the entry by himself so that you don't need to accompany him right up to the first few poles.

In training, proofing weave entries is fundamental. For example, your dog needs to learn to decelerate for the weave entry even if you are not slowing down. This is difficult for your dog, and it's worth observing that many top handlers show some deceleration during competition as their dog drives towards the weave entry.

Consider the words you use to cue a weave for your dog. Is your verbal cue clearly distinct from your other cues? Do you tend to add in other words as well, for example "go"? If you do, think about whether this might be confusing for your dog. What should your dog do in response to the cue "go" normally? And if there is a weave entry beside an off-course jump, how will your dog discriminate between the two?

HOW TO TRAIN WEAVE ENTRIES

- When you are working around the imaginary clock-face, consider your handling as a clue, but not the answer. Your feet and shoulders can face towards the entry, but avoid moving towards the entry (it's best to stay static), and use minimal or no arm movement. Make sure you work with your dog on both sides.

Start with two poles, and work close to them. Position yourself and your dog side-by-side and do a little shaping with your dog, preferably using chunks of food. Keep your feet still during this process. Pay particular attention to your reward position. Throw the rewards so that your dog associates them with his behaviour through the poles rather than you – do not give them from your hand. Make sure you work with your dog on both sides of you so he learns to find the entry regardless of your position.

Gradually work your way around an imaginary clock-face so that your dog is learning to enter the two poles from a variety of angles.

- Once your dog is becoming really proficient at the game, add your verbal cue.

Progressions

- Continue to vary your dog's angle of approach.
- Gradually add in varied handler movement (acceleration, deceleration and a variety of speeds).
- Vary your start position and direction of travel.
- Vary which side of you your dog is on.
- Vary the distance of your dog from the entry, which will also vary his speed of approach.
- Vary the location in which you train your weave entries. Move the two poles around your garden, for example, and take them to a range of parks or agility venues.
- Introduce visual distractions (e.g. dogs nearby or agility obstacles near the weave entry).
- Work with weaves that look different (including different colour weave poles).

- Try some entries which do not allow you to be nearby – for example, where your dog is emerging from a tunnel into the weave and is well ahead of you.

- Do some entries on a greater number of weave poles, including working on up to 12 poles. Continue to reward the weave entry, using a verbal cue such as "find it" to tell your dog to search out his treat or toy after two or three poles, rather than completing all 12.

- Do some entries which are preceded by short sequences.

COMMON ENTRY PROBLEMS

Weave entry problems can be caused by physical issues. Consult your dog's healthcare provider before embarking on a training programme to fix a weave entry problem.

Weaving is physically and mentally demanding so work with just two or three poles when you are teaching entries.

Q. My dog does not decelerate enough for the weave entry.

- Your dog succeeds more frequently when the speed of approach is slower.
- Your dog may run past the weaves altogether, or may enter the weaves only to skip one or more poles near the beginning.

What is going on

Straight approaches can be harder than they appear. Your dog needs to anticipate the entry and change his behaviour accordingly before reaching them, typically by decelerating. Bigger dogs will need to collect more than smaller dogs on fast, straight entries. Some straight approaches do not allow your dog to see the weaves for very long in advance of needing to do them – for instance when travelling to them out of a curved tunnel or after a wall jump.

- Your dog may not have enough experience to have learnt how, and when, to decelerate for faster weave entries (particularly outside of his familiar training environment).
- The information you give your dog may be too late, or insufficient, so he doesn't get enough warning to be able to respond.
- Your dog may not be very motivated to slow down to find the entry as not enough value has been placed on what he may otherwise consider a boring behaviour.

Fixing it

- Do entry work which incorporates straight entries.
- Do a lot of rewarding at the weave entry, being very conscious of the reward position. Reward at pole two or three, and never throw the reward forward of your dog. In comparison, rewarding for the completion of 12 poles should be minimal.
- In training, incrementally increase your dog's speed of approach.
- In training, incrementally increase your movement so that your

dog learns how to nail the entry even when you show motion and acceleration.

- In the short term, in a trial setting when you want to help your dog succeed, consider decelerating as your dog nears the weave part of the course so that his success and confidence in that environment is raised.

Q. When my dog is approaching from the side of the weaves where he needs to keep one pole to his left, he does not consistently identify the correct entry.

What is going on

Finding this type of entry accurately is really difficult. Other obstacles nearby can intensify the challenge. It takes plenty of training to teach your dog how to do this behaviour correctly.

Your dog may be thinking that wrapping a pole, on his right, is what leads to him being rewarded, and may not have realised that he needs a single pole on his left. This leaves him with multiple potential entry positions.

Fixing it

- Work on these approaches, rewarding at the entry. Be sure to do so on a 12-pole weave, too (still rewarding at the entry) when your dog is consistently successful with fewer poles.

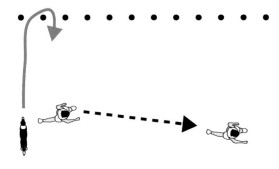

To make sure your dog really understands his job, try moving away from the weave entry as he drives towards it. Can he still complete the job, despite the distraction?

- Be very aware of your own body language. If you are using your body to push your dog into the weaves he will not learn how to find the entry without that clue. Avoid unconsciously 'helping' too much during training. Try deliberately facing your feet and shoulders towards the middle or end of the weave as he approaches the entry.

- Vary the weave location frequently, as well as the surrounding obstacles and the angle and speed of approach.

- Gradually precede the entry with short sequences, but continue to reward.

Q. On sharp angles, my dog heads to the correct entry position at first but then does not turn sufficiently to come back in for the next pole.

What is going on

This is a common problem, especially with bigger dogs, and particularly when the dog is approaching at high speed. To turn back into the weaves correctly, the dog needs to be super-fit, to be able to load individual limbs with his bodyweight and to have plenty of value in the behaviour so that he will want to put in the huge effort required.

Fixing it

- Present your dog with challenges replicating the one he finds hard. Start close up and gradually increase the speed of his approach.

- Be very aware of your reward position – make sure it is at pole two or three and is such that your dog has to slow, and turn significantly, to get his reward.

- In training, work towards your dog understanding how to nail the entry even when you show lots of movement and acceleration towards the entry, just when he needs to slow down.

- In the short term, in a trial setting when you want to help your dog succeed, consider decelerating as your dog nears the weave entry part of the course so that his confidence is raised by success in that environment.

I was attending a training camp with lots of other handlers. One of the handlers had won the world championship several times, and was a top trainer and competitor. She was working her dog, and they were doing the weaves as part of a sequence.

Her dog drove into the entrance beautifully, but she pulled her out and set her at the weaves again. The same thing happened again, and again...

By this time we were all looking at each other quizzically, wondering what she was correcting. It seemed a great behaviour to us. The trainer intervened, asking what the handler wasn't happy with. Oops – she had had a momentarily mind blank and thought her dog was getting the entry wrong!

This sort of mistake happens to all of us at some point. We aren't perfect. There will be times during training when you realise that what you have been doing hasn't been quite right for one reason or another. Don't give yourself a hard time for it. It happens to the best people.

WEAVE INDEPENDENCE

What if your dog doesn't weave accurately when you get ahead of him? If he won't allow you to change sides while he weaves, or comes out when you peel away? Rest assured your dog can learn how to do all these behaviours and more – he just needs to be taught how to do so.

Teaching weave independence helps your dog understand his weave job better. What's more, it makes weaves much easier for you to handle in sequences.

Once great weave independence is achieved, you will be able to tackle some very tricky challenges together. You will be able to take the most efficient line for you as a handler since you won't need to stay alongside your dog in order for him to correctly navigate his way through the poles.

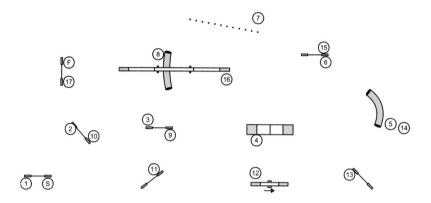

In this sequence it would be extremely inconvenient for you to travel to the end of the poles with your dog – much better, instead, if you can get to the other side of the dog-walk ready to cue obstacles 9, 10, 11, 12.

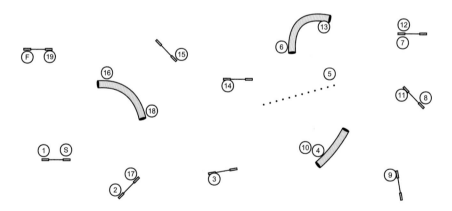

In this sequence, it would be much easier to send your dog into the weaves and head directly over to obstacle 6. If you are unable to get there before your dog has done the weaves, handling the next section of the sequence will be challenging.

While your dog weaves, there may be things that you need to be doing on course such as:

- Being far ahead of your dog.
- Being far behind your dog.
- Moving away from your dog.
- Accelerating.
- Decelerating.
- Blind/front crossing before he completes the weaves.
- Rear crossing (crossing behind) before he completes the weaves.
- Crossing over the weave line (serping them).
- Layering obstacles (handling at a distance, sometimes behind other obstacles) as your dog weaves.

The dog learns to complete the weaves, even though he may be receiving instructions of where to go next.

Photo: Matt Bowen for www.winclinic.co.uk

HOW TO TRAIN INDEPENDENT WEAVES

When training independence, your first job is to make the rest of your dog's weave job relatively straightforward. That means a simple entry. It could also mean working with, for example, slightly channelled weaves, or at the outset using six weaves and then transferring to 12 once the behaviour is understood.

This set-up will help you introduce weave independence exercises to your dog.

The tunnel allows your dog to present to the weave from the same angle and speed every time – making the entry easy.

The jump should be set on the lowest possible height and be positioned a comfortable, easy distance (such as 7 metres/22ft) from the weave exit. This positioning gives your dog a forward focus after the weaves and will help discourage him from looking at you near the weave exit. You will probably want to cue the jump verbally as your dog completes the weaves, for example saying "go!"

You can use a static reward (such as a treat dispenser or dead toy) on the floor after the jump, or you can use a thrown reward (thrown to land on the floor after the dog has committed to the jump). As your training progresses, it makes sense to mix it up between the two types of reward. The static reward helps your dog succeed – but it will not be there in competition.

- Start with three or four successful, easy repetitions of the exercise (see above). Behave as you would, normally, while your dog weaves (for example, travel alongside him at a steady pace). This step is your safe anchor. If you start to hit too many failures during the next exercises, return to this step and repeat it before returning to the independence challenge you are working on.

- Reduce your movement, becoming gradually more still as your dog weaves. Begin by moving more slowly, progress to being completely static the whole time your dog weaves.

- Try decelerating as your dog weaves. Begin smoothly and, gradually, progress to being more abrupt.

- Stay parallel to, but further away than normal, from the weaves. Build up the distance.

- Try peeling away diagonally from the weaves as your dog completes them. Gradually increase the angle and distance.

- Be ahead of your dog while he weaves. Initially, do this by sending to the tunnel so that you are already further forward than you would normally be when he exits the tunnel. That way, you don't have to add in lots of movement. Keep rewarding in the same place; don't reward further forward just because you are now ahead of him.

- Accelerate as your dog weaves.

- Combine the two previous steps: starting further ahead, and accelerating as your dog weaves.

- Work towards being able to travel in the opposite direction as your dog weaves. Begin by just turning slightly to face towards the tunnel. Gradually start to travel towards the tunnel while your dog is in the weaves. Increase the distance you are travelling, and your speed, when you are ready. This is more than a cool party trick. It will be useful for some of the next exercises, where you will be starting to head in a very contrary direction to the direction of your dog.

- Repeat the previous exercise but as you move from one side of the weaves to the other, carry out a front or blind cross while your dog is mid-weave. So if he started the weaves on your left, by the time he completes them he is on your right. Slowly work on adding in progressions: travelling further, faster and on sharper angles.

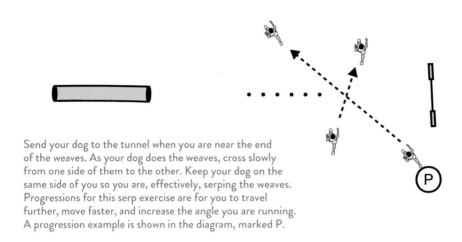

Send your dog to the tunnel when you are near the end of the weaves. As your dog does the weaves, cross slowly from one side of them to the other. Keep your dog on the same side of you so you are, effectively, serping the weaves. Progressions for this serp exercise are for you to travel further, move faster, and increase the angle you are running. A progression example is shown in the diagram, marked P.

- Cross behind your dog as he weaves. To begin, position yourself near the tunnel exit and travel parallel to the weaves, just slotting in a subtle swap from one side of your dog to the other as he drives ahead of you through the weaves. You can make this harder by crossing over more abruptly, and by changing the angles so you are on more acute diagonal lines, rather than parallel.

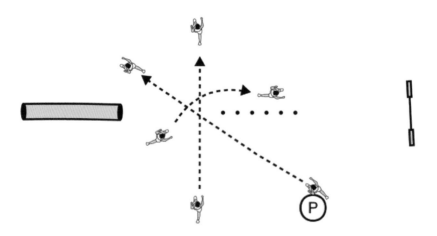

An example of a harder cross behind is marked with a P.

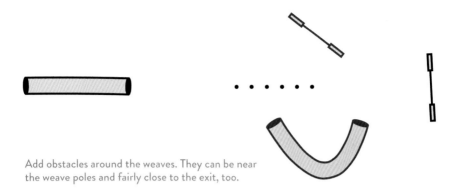

Add obstacles around the weaves. They can be near the weave poles and fairly close to the exit, too.

Once your dog is awesome at all the independence exercises, you can gradually transition the skills you have both rehearsed away from this set-up and into sequences, continuing to reward frequently to reinforce the independence.

The next step is to test the independence out at a different training venue or at a simulated competition event. In time, you will have the confidence to use that independence in the ring.

Q. My dog comes out at the 10th weave pole. What should I do?

What is going on

Coming out early (often around pole 10) is a common weave issue, especially in the early days of your dog's weave training. The weave independence exercises will contribute to solving this issue.

One of the key things to be aware of when fixing 10 pole-itis is how you reward. Sometimes the dog comes out because:

- He anticipates the reward being thrown at the end of the weaves.
- You burrow in your pocket or retract your arm at around this point, ready to toss in the reward.
- Your dog has learnt to look at you and then get his reward (thus being rewarded for looking at you, which is the behaviour he then offers towards the end of the weaves).

- You throw the reward to one side or other of the weaves, or deliver it from your hand, so the dog wants to drive in that direction rather than focusing on travelling forward out of the weaves.

Fixing it

- Add an obstacle after the weaves (such as a very low height jump) which the dog is taught to drive towards after the weave, before his reward arrives.

- Ask someone else to throw your reward.

- Do lots of weaves to a static reward, which is already positioned out ahead of the weaves. You may sometimes want to hide it, for example in longer grass.

Q. Should I clap while my dog is in the weaves? Should I keep saying my weave cue or be quiet once he is in them?

What is going on

There is nothing wrong with giving additional encouragement or cues while your dog weaves, and it may help maximise your dog's speed. However, sometimes handlers only give additional cues when they are doing something they feel uneasy about (such as pulling away from the weaves). This should be avoided – it tends to have the opposite of the desired effect and highlights that something out of the ordinary is happening.

Fixing it

Vary what you do in training so your dog is not reliant on additional cues in order to continue weaving.

- Avoid giving additional cues to keep your dog on task when you are moving off, or completing a move which may distract him. It generally has the opposite of the desired effect.

- Additional cues can be useful in situations where your dog is weaving with beautiful independence but you are, to some extent, out of his sightline and he needs to be aware of your new position before exiting the weaves.

Q. What should I do if my dog makes a weave mistake?

What is going on

Allowing your dog to continue through the weaves after an error can tire him if it's happening repeatedly. It can also make it harder for your dog to understand the fault since, by the time he realises he isn't being rewarded, it may be a second or so after the mistake.

Fixing it

If an error has occurred – such as an incorrect entry or a missed step mid-weave – it helps if you have a calm, quiet cue that asks your dog to stop weaving

- Avoid using your body to tell your dog he has gone wrong. For example, let's say he mis-steps at pole five. If you simply walk back to the start of the weaves at that point, pulling your dog with you, you may inadvertently teach your dog to mimic your body language. He will be learning that if you pull away from the weaves, he should pull out of them with you. This is undesirable and makes training independence more difficult. In this situation a verbal cue, which marks the fact that the dog should stop weaving, is really useful.

- The dog can then be re-presented with the task and, if necessary, the challenge can be diminished so that the dog succeeds quickly.

Remember that weaves are a super-challenging behaviour for your dog. Keep your expectations fair. Your dog's weave entries and independence at training need to be awesome for them to be good in competition. Reward your dog's weave behaviours often.

Chapter Eight
CONTACT SKILLS

*"To get great contacts, you need to know your dog
and apply the method in a way that is most suitable for
your dog, as an individual."*

Anne Lenz

Contact performances have become faster and faster over the years. Running contacts are now commonplace, especially at the top level of competition.

Judging super speedy contact performances is not easy. Occasionally, electronic sensors are used to assist judges. In some organisations there are both on and off contact judges – especially for the dog-walk. Most organisations, however, still have a single judge responsible for marking the on and off. One or two organisations have deemed the on contact obsolete.

Contact equipment varies. The degree to which it bounces, what material is used for the surface and for the trestles, how many supports it has, how the end planks taper to meet the floor, how quickly the seesaw tips, and so on. Dogs have to assess all of this at speed in a competition environment and adjust immediately in order to deliver the contact behaviour they have been taught.

Running contacts and stop contacts are the two commonly trained behaviours.

Contact equipment provides a challenge for dogs – and judges!

Photo: Matt Bowen
for www.winclinic.co.uk

RUNNING CONTACTS

The A-frame and dog-walk

Running contacts have become increasingly common, and although they are tough for the dog to perform, they have also become so well trained that they are increasingly accurate.

What's great about running contacts?

- In some scenarios, running contacts are definitely faster than quick-released stop contacts. The time gained is not just across the contact but also after the contact, since the dog maintains his speed as he approaches the obstacles that follow.

- Handling your dog when he has a running contact can be a lot of fun. It can feel amazing to run alongside your dog as he fires across the dog-walk at lightning speed.

- When you have stop contacts, you typically need to do a percentage of training runs. These are runs in a competition environment, during which you do not cue a quick-release. They are done to ensure your dog maintains the trained stop behaviour. You don't need to do this in the same way with running contacts. Although you do need to be consistent in your approach, the behaviour you want your dog to deliver when he has a running contact is the same during training as during a competition final.

- Running contacts may well be easier on your dog's body over time. Although they encourage your dog to travel at high speed, the movement is more continuous and there is not the demand to rapidly decelerate that is needed with a stop.

Any downsides to running contacts?

- Handling a running contact is not always easy, especially a running dog-walk. You may find that you have to handle from a greater distance or run faster before, during or after the contact. In addition, you will not have the momentary pause during a run that stop contacts can provide. However, agility is a speed sport where time advantages are continually sought – and that's a big part of the fun of it.

- Running contacts are not the easiest behaviour to train. A-frames are far more straightforward to teach than dog-walks. With running contact training you are not teaching a single, standalone behaviour as you are with a stop. Instead, your dog will need to learn to deal with different scenarios after the contact (such as tight turns and discrimination) as an integral part of that running behaviour.

- Teaching running contacts to dogs as a retrain (for example, to dogs who previously had a stop contact behaviour) can be much harder than training them from the outset. The dog will have become accustomed to certain movement patterns, such as decelerating on the down plank of the dog-walk, and this has to be unlearnt.

- Any underlying physical causes of variation in striding can complicate running contacts. For example, dogs who have issues, such as grades of patella luxation, can have intermittent hind limb extension and this can affect their consistency.

Understanding running A-frames

Most dogs are relatively quick to learn a successful running A-frame behaviour.

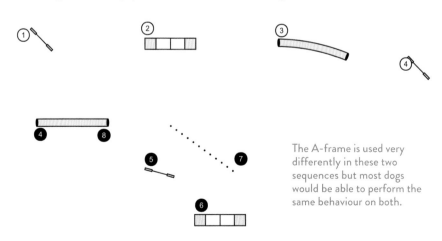

The A-frame is used very differently in these two sequences but most dogs would be able to perform the same behaviour on both.

A running A-frame is a lot easier to master than a dog-walk because most dogs can perform the A-frame similarly, regardless of its position in the course.

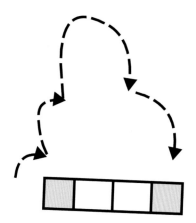

The majority of dogs can comfortably learn a behaviour in which the dog hits the A-frame in four positions while travelling over it. Longer striding dogs may sometimes be more at ease with a variation in which only three hits are made – either two on the up and one on the down, or one on the up and two on the down.

Understanding running dog-walks

The way a dog performs a running dog-walk will be different depending on its position on the course.

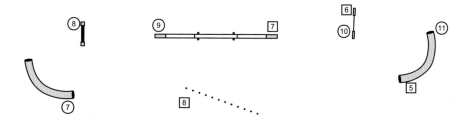

Turning tightly off the end of the dog-walk, for example into the weaves, necessitates collection and deceleration on the down plank. In contrast, driving forward after the contact to the jump, and tunnel, allows for extension and acceleration across the entire dog-walk.

Running contacts: The dog maintains speed and momentum, and can move off fluently to the next obstacle.

Photos: Matt Bowen
for www.winclinic.co.uk

HOW TO TRAIN RUNNING CONTACTS

A-frame and dog-walk

Several methods can be used to train running contacts, and there are benefits to each. Some dogs are better suited to one method than another; you can also combine multiple methods. Fit and more body-aware dogs will find running contact behaviours easier to acquire.

TARGET METHOD

With this method, you begin by shaping your dog to target something with his feet – for example, a rubber, square mat. After this behaviour is perfected, the target is transferred to the area of the contact you want your dog to touch. Eventually the target is removed, intermittently, once the habit of touching that area of contact is well established.

133

The benefits

- This method is useful for helping your dog to get a mental understanding of the running criteria.
- It works well with dogs who flourish with shaping.
- It is useful for teaching the unique footwork required on particular turns since the target provides a clear and specific point for the dog to aim to hit.

The target used must have good grip and be well secured when it is on the contact.

The key to success is to start by doing plenty of games, and proofing, with the target as a groundwork exercise. A plus point is that you can work with a youngster since training can begin relatively early. Only transfer the target to the dog-walk or A-frame once your dog is adept at playing target games on the flat.

The target must have good grip and be well secured when it is on the contact.

STRIDING METHOD

This method begins with running. The dog is encouraged to run with full extension and speed from the outset. Once this is happening over a flat plank, the handler jackpots good hits on the off-contact.

Using this method, understanding is added once the speed is already there. It probably works best with dogs who have a naturally low, extended running movement. Dogs with less consistent running patterns (whether a result of their conformation or any other cause) may find this method more challenging.

REGULATOR METHOD

Regulators are used to prevent your dog touching specific areas of the dog-walk or A-frame. This makes a desired stride pattern more likely and, thereby, increases the chance that your dog will touch the contact area in the way you want.

They are often of value at the formative stage – when your dog is developing a habit of how he will do the dog-walk or A-frame. However, they do not directly 'explain' the mental demand of a running contact to your dog.

In time, it is essential to teach your dog how to perform his contacts in the absence of regulators, i.e. intermittently removing them and rewarding for maintenance of the behaviour.

The regulator method may be combined with the other methods outlined above.

Regulators can be used effectively to minimise failure.

RUNNING CONTACT SCENARIOS

There are a variety of exit scenarios to consider in relation to training a running contact. Here are some of the most commonly used scenarios.

- Straight-ish exits where the dog continues forward after the contact to a tunnel or jump obstacle.
- Soft turns off the contact towards the next obstacle.
- Tight turns off the contact where the dog turns back on himself.
- Exits requiring the dog to turn away from the handler's direction.

Some handlers train only one, or a few, scenarios as running contact behaviours, and additionally train a stop which they cue when working one of the other scenarios.

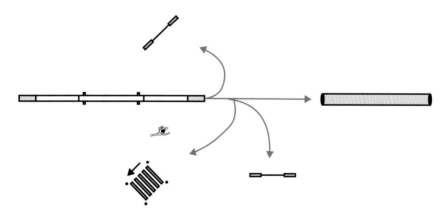

Training for running contacts can cover a variety of possible exits.

PROOFING RUNNING CONTACTS

As with all behaviours in agility, making running contacts really solid requires proofing and generalisation. This means maintaining and rewarding the behaviour as you gradually vary the circumstances, for example:

- Varying handler movement and position.

- Incorporating front, blind and rear crosses.

- Doing a range of approaches to the contact, as well as a range of exits.

- Covering a number of environments and a variety of suppliers' equipment.

Accurate running dog-walks are physically demanding. Unusual patterns of behaviour, or changes in performance, can often be indicative of even very slight injuries. Consult a canine health professional when this is a possibility.

THE ON-CONTACT

Few dogs naturally miss the on-contact, so it is far less frequently trained than the off-contact. As you begin training your contacts, keep an eye on your dog's typical on contact behaviour. A minority of dogs will regularly miss – typically those with very long strides. These dogs may be taught on-contact criteria, using the same kinds of methods as with the off-contact.

STOP CONTACTS

A-frame and dog-walk

The principle behind a stop contact is to teach your dog to pause in a specific position on the off-contact until you give a release cue. The idea is that when you really need to go for time, you can release him as he drives into that position – thus achieving a fast and accurate contact.

When training stop contacts, aim for independence. With an independent stop contact, your dog is able to drive down into his stop position on his own, ignoring your body language. He doesn't need you to be near the end of the contact, nor does he need you to decelerate as he nears the stop position. He understands how to perform the behaviour by himself. If you stop while the dog is halfway along the contact, he will continue at speed to the end and stop. If you race past the end, he will stop confidently in position rather than following you. Not needing to manage the contact behaviour with your body language frees you to take the most efficient route around the course.

A variety of stop positions can be taught. The most common is 2on, 2off – where your dog is taught to stop at the bottom of the contact with his hindlimbs on the contact and his forelimbs on the floor. When training this position, aim for your dog to be fairly low on the contact.

The 2on, 2off position at the end of the contact.

Other common stop positions are:

4on – the dog stops near the end of the contact with all four feet still on the off contact.

4off – the dog stops near the end of the contact with all four feet on the floor, sometimes in a down.

HOW TO TRAIN STOP CONTACTS

Your dog needs to have a good awareness of his back end for all contact behaviours, including stop contacts. Initially, it's helpful to train your stop behaviour somewhere other than on a contact. Get hold of, or make, something like a block (see below). Check the surface has great grip and is appropriate to the size and height of your dog. This means that you can perfect the behaviour, and the understanding, away from real agility kit, and only bring it to equipment once you are both feeling competent and confident.

Keep practising until your dog becomes familiar with the 2on 2off position.

Before beginning, plan how to reward. Reward location is really important when training a stop contact. You want your dog to associate the reward with *his* position, not *your* position. He needs to want to be in place on the block (and eventually at the end of the contact) rather than opting to follow your hand or to just be where you are.

When using treats for your stop contacts, it's useful to deliver them by dropping them on the floor. Sometimes they might be in place before your dog arrives in position, ready for him to find. Other times you might place them after your dog has stopped. Avoid encouraging him to eat treats out of your hand. Keep your hands non-distracting during stop contact games – maybe even behind your back – so that your dog isn't learning to stare at them.

Similarly, when using a toy as the reward, vary how you deliver it. Sometimes leave it on the ground for your dog to find, in position. Other times, throw it to him, in position, after he's stopped.

You may want to play tug with your dog while he is in a 2on 2off. This is useful for adding value to the place you want him to love. If he hasn't done static tugging before, he is likely to move out of position during the game. That's fine; very gradually build up to tugging with him in position by making the game most fun when he is where you want him to be. Be aware of how your position, and the way you hold the toy during a tug game, will influence your dog. For example, if you stand to one side of your dog when tugging it may pull him off the contact when he tries to pull away from you. It's easiest for your dog if you grip the toy firmly, with both hands, and stand directly facing him during the tug game.

To build value in the stop position, you can add the criteria of the dog looking down to the ground before rewarding. You can use a small, visible target to train this, which the dog is encouraged to touch with his nose or mouth.

Your dog may need some encouragement to play when he is in the 2on 2off position.

- Lure or shape your dog into something approaching the position you want him to adopt on the block. Be informal and easy-going. Make it a super fun place for your dog to be – deliver lots of rewards whenever your dog is more or less in the position you are working towards.

- Initially, your dog will quickly move out of position. Just do the really fun rewarding when he is where you want him to be. Gradually, work towards rewarding, pausing briefly, and then rewarding a few more times so that your dog learns to remain in position, awaiting a further reward.

- Over time, start to increase the pause. You can then start to introduce a release which triggers movement out of the contact position. If your dog has already learned a great release during your start-line training, that might be the easiest one to begin with.

- The next step is to work towards your dog racing into position. Gradually build up the distance your dog needs to travel to drive into position. Do this incrementally, as it is difficult for him. The aim is for him to learn how to move into his stop at speed, so that he only needs to decelerate fairly late. Alternate the first reward – sometimes put it ready for your dog to find on the floor as he reaches position, sometimes give it to him after he has stopped in position. Follow up the first reward with more rewards, with variable pauses between them. Then release.

When training stop contacts, there is always a balance to be struck between speed and accuracy. Remember that being fast is as important as being correct in agility. If your dog overshoots his position during the early stages of training, remember that's happened because he's trying to be quick – and that's a good thing!

Progressions

- The next phase is to vary your position and movement as a handler. Here are some things to cover for your body language proofing. Do these as your dog drives into position on his block:

  - Stay behind your dog and let him go well ahead of you.

  - Race past your dog.

  - Move diagonally away.

  - Cross behind him.

  - Blind/front cross ahead of him.

- Now transfer the behaviour to the contact. To do this, lower the contact you are using as much as possible. Ask for your stop behaviour on the block, which should be positioned beside the contact. Then hide the block and ask your dog to hop on to the off-contact (he doesn't need to do the full piece of equipment). Encourage him to find the same position on the contact as he found on the block.

When you transfer the behaviour, start working with a low plank.

- Slowly work through all the games you played with the block, but now play them on the off-contact. Build up to asking your dog to do the full piece of equipment on very low height. Take your time and stay consistent.

- Finally, slowly raise the height of the equipment. If you did the groundwork on the block really well, this stage should be relatively plain sailing.

- You are now ready to put your contact into sequences. Continue to reward often, and to vary your position as described in the progression list.

TAKING STOP CONTACTS INTO COMPETITION

When you initially take your stop contacts into more challenging environments, such as competition, the behaviour will be more difficult for your dog. The contacts may look visually different, they

143

may perform differently, and there will be lots of distractions. It is important to give your dog a reasonable chance of success, without introducing inconsistency.

In competition, it often helps if you move relatively slowly as your dog learns to find his stop position. The key is to keep your pace constant for at least three seconds before, and three seconds after, your dog finds position. Don't decelerate at the moment your dog should be stopping. Think of your body language as making your dog less likely to fail, but not giving him the answer. Never slow down, or stop, just when he needs to stop. Travel at a constant pace – just make it a relatively slow pace. Once your dog has built up a little bank of success in a variety of environments, it then becomes feasible to move more quickly as your dog does his stop contacts.

Decide on a strategy for the ring, and rehearse this strategy in training as well:

"If my dog doesn't stop I will..."

"If my dog stops beautifully I will..."

"If my dog stops beautifully, but releases before I say the word I will..."

Show your dog strategies that are consistent across environments, and he will respond with a consistent behaviour in return.

Q. Why are my stop contacts slow?

What is going on

Stops are physically challenging. Your dog has to be happy to run down the equivalent of a hill whilst in complete control of his body, and land in something akin to a press up, in order to deliver a stop. He needs to be comfortable loading his front end; dogs with straight fronts, such as Fox Terriers, may find this especially hard.

Fixing it

Remember, your dog needs to be warmed up and as physically fit as possible. Talk to your canine health professional about what factors may affect your dog and how you can better prepare him for stops.

What is going on

Doing too many repetitions where you travel ahead as your dog reaches his stop position may lead him to think that the criteria involves waiting for you to go past him. Equally, releasing your dog before he has fully reached his stop position can make him decelerate too soon, anticipating your cue to go. Typically, these issues are characterised by the dog slowing on the last plank and glancing at you. They can also be associated with a stalking type movement.

Fixing it

Concentrate on teaching your dog to love driving right down into position with you well behind him, out of his line of vision. Don't add yourself back into the equation until he is racing down to the end; consider yourself as a distraction you want your dog to ignore. Only release your dog after he has found position.

What is going on

It could be that your dog is not entirely sure of the behaviour you want from him, and believes you are likely to be unhappy with his performance. Unsure of the desired position, he worries and travels slowly for a longer period of time in an attempt not to get it wrong. This is often associated with a handler who has, historically, prioritised accuracy over speed. So if the dog reached position (albeit slowly), the handler would be content. If the dog was fast over the contact, but missed position, the handler would not be happy and would ask the dog to redo some, or all, of the contact. The dog would then, in all likelihood, respond by travelling more slowly than the first time, but the handler would be pleased because the accuracy had improved. Therefore, the dog learns that his handler wants him to go slowly.

Fixing it

First, appreciate that speed is as important as accuracy. With cautious dogs, or those with a tendency to be anxious, care has to be taken when upping the difficulty level of stop contacts. Your dog needs to be extremely likely to succeed at all times during any kind of retrain. The excitement and fun in contacts needs to be found, which may mean experimenting with the reward strategy and rethinking what to do when the behaviour isn't as desired.

Q. Why are my stop contacts good in training and not at a show?

What is going on

Over-arousal. Your dog is generally over-aroused in a show environment; the loss of his stop criteria is just one manifestation of his inability to manage the increase in stress and excitement. Typically, other behaviours weaken in line with this. He may generally appear more wound up at competition. He may be more likely to knock poles or to bark. He may be less likely to perform a start-line wait. He may display reactivity or over-excitement in the run up to his turn in the ring.

Fixing it

Your focus should be on generally reducing your dog's arousal both on a daily basis and, eventually, specifically in a show environment. You need to work on this before you re-attempt success in the ring. A behaviourist or trainer may be helpful. Create a strategy for taking your dog from your vehicle to the ring in a way that prepares him for running, without elevating his arousal. Increase the self-control behaviours your dog performs on a daily basis, as well as at a showground. Make those behaviours valuable to your dog. Be aware that physical issues can also cause over-arousal.

What is going on

Unreliable contacts in the ring could also be because your dog feels insecure in a show environment. In this case, the issue with contacts is unlikely to be the only evidence of his emotional state. He may show signs such as having his ears further back, and his tail lower down, than normal, and he may look around warily.

Fixing it

Work on your dog's general comfort around anything which seems to trigger this – it could be the presence of other dogs, certain noises, and so on. A behaviourist or trainer may be able to help. Depending on the severity, your dog may need a break from agility or from competitions. You may, with care, be able to increase exposure to the source of his discomfort at training, provided you can do so while maintaining and building his confidence. Reducing day-to-day stressors in his life may be crucial.

What is going on

You may be over-supporting your dog by decelerating or stopping when your dog is nearing the contact area. You have therefore taught your dog to watch your body to tell him what he is meant to do.

Fixing it

Watch some videos of you, and your dog, doing stop contacts both in training and at competition. Are you travelling at a constant pace as your dog nears his stop position, or is there a change in your body language? Focus on keeping your movement continuous and constant as your dog nears his position, so that he learns not to look to you for information about his behaviour.

What is going on

You tend to associate the movement of your body with your 'verbal' release cue so your dog has learned an incorrect behaviour.

Fixing it

Again, use live footage of your stop contacts in training and in competition. Mute the sound. Can you still tell when you release your dog? If so, your movement is the release cue rather than your verbal cue. You are teaching your dog to watch you closely and to mimic your body language on contacts. This means when you move forward your dog will not want to stop, and he will be unclear when he is expected to release. Focus on keeping your body absolutely constant while you release him so that the only thing that he can possibly interpret as a release cue is your verbal one. Video your sessions so you can check on your body language.

What is going on

You are inconsistent in show environments, compared to how you are in training. When you are training, you have a clear strategy for what you do if your dog's contact performance is not what you want. If he comes off, you may redo the whole contact, or even the whole sequence. Now, in training, he rarely comes off. In the ring, you feel the pressure of others watching and of taking up the judge's time. Plus you want to get a clear round, so a pre-emptive release by your dog – which you wouldn't allow in training – is ignored in the ring. Either way, your behaviour in the ring is different to your behaviour at training. Your dog mimics you – his behaviour in the ring is different to his behaviour at training.

Fixing it

Decide on a strategy which you are happy to adopt across both training and competition for your stop contacts. Write down what you will do if your dog nails his contact. What you will do if he comes off early. What you will do if he doesn't stop at all, and so on. Fix this note somewhere prominent, such as on your fridge or your dashboard. Now stick to this criteria – both at training and at competition. It will take a while to change the behaviour you accidentally taught your dog to do in the ring, but it is achievable. It may be easier if you start by going to simulated competitions so that you can initially rehearse your in-ring behaviours in a less pressured environment.

What is going on

Your dog is becoming increasingly confused about what he is meant to be doing, and he is worried about failing. This will slow some dogs down, but others will go quicker and rush off the contact when they anticipate disappointment in their behaviour.

Fixing it

Focus on making your stop contacts rock solid. Keep your movement constant when your dog needs to stop, and when you release him. Be consistent across training and competition. Praise and reward your dog heavily in contact position – and when you are both ready, go to some simulated competitions where you can praise and reward in the ring, as well.

THE SEESAW

The seesaw incorporates the unique challenge of a tipping movement into the contact equipment. Your dog needs to be on the seesaw when it touches the ground, as well as touching the on- and off-contact as he traverses it.

Physically, the seesaw is tough on your dog so don't start training on the actual equipment until he is well developed. Your dog needs to run at speed, rapidly decelerate and absorb the force of the landing before pushing off in a forward direction.

PREPARATION

Before working with a seesaw, prepare your dog for the challenge by getting him used to the feeling of movement beneath him. Introduce him to wobble boards, and to behaviours such as closing doors or pushing a skateboard along, rewarding and reinforcing him so you build a positive association

In separate sessions, gradually accustom your dog to the noise a seesaw makes when it hits the floor so that he perceives this noise to be welcome and positive.

Foundation training is key to negotiating the seesaw.

HOW TO TRAIN THE SEESAW

You can teach your dog to run through the contact on a seesaw, although the majority of competitors train the seesaw as a stop behaviour.

With a running seesaw, your dog will still need to pause momentarily on the end of the seesaw, but rather than stopping in a specific position, he is taught to continue once it touches the floor. This is most commonly trained using a hoop on the ground, immediately after the seesaw, which the dog is taught to run through after completing the seesaw.

It can be hard to get accuracy with a hoop since it never exists in a

Use a jump wing to support the up-plank of the seesaw while
your dog is learning to go into position.

competition setting, making the behaviour a bit 'grey'. In addition,
most handlers want to have a stop contact in their armoury in case
running A-frames and dog-walks don't go to plan.

A stop behaviour on the seesaw involves dogs, typically, adopting a
2-on 2-off position. Smaller, lighter dogs may be trained a 4-on.

- Teach a stop behaviour in your chosen position away from the
  contact equipment (see page 139).

- If you have an adjustable seesaw, begin on the lowest height
  setting.

- Raise the on-contact part of the seesaw (for example by propping
  it on a jump wing) so that the off-contact is only a fraction off the
  ground.

- Shape your dog to touch the off-contact part of the seesaw. As
  soon as he touches the seesaw, toss a treat away from it.

- Once your dog is happily touching the seesaw with a paw, deliver
  a treat to him in that position. Wait for him to pause there for a
  moment, and then toss another treat away from the seesaw.

- Build up the number of paws your dog has on the seesaw, until he is leaping on with all four feet. Do lots of rewarding while your dog is on the seesaw. Give one, or no treats after he has got off the seesaw – this will help make being on the seesaw a very valuable place to be.

- Gradually add the stop contact behaviour you have taught away from the seesaw. For example, if you have taught the behaviour on a block, position the block near the seesaw and do two successful repetitions on the block. Then hide the block and repeat the stop behaviour using the off-contact part of the seesaw.

- Raise the height of the off-contact part of the seesaw fractionally from the ground, but only to the point where it is still safe for your dog to jump on to the side. Repeat the stop behaviour. Once your dog has nailed this, he will have learnt to become accustomed to the unstable tipping motion of the seesaw.

- The next step is to teach your dog to race up a plank – since the object is for your dog to drive right to the end of the seesaw before it tips. To start, put the seesaw on its lowest possible height, and position the on-contact end of the seesaw on the ground. The off-contact part of the seesaw should be positioned on something like a very low table with a non-slip surface. The seesaw should only be able to tip very slightly, or not at all.

- Encourage your dog to run up the low plank and on to the table. Do lots of rewarding on the table, so your dog wants to get up there as soon as possible. Repeat until your dog is confident enough to race up the plank to the table.

- Gradually incorporate your stop position criteria into the game, at the end of the seesaw plank on the table.

- Increase the drop to the table by tiny degrees.

- Diminish the height of the table, using smaller platforms, until the plank is dropping to the floor.

- Gradually increase the height of the seesaw until it is at full height.

- Work on progression games for stop contacts (see page 142).

PART III
THE AGILITY HANDLER

Chapter Nine

HANDLING

"A dog doesn't care if you're rich or poor, educated or illiterate, clever or dull. Give him your heart and he will give you his."

John Grogan

There is no right way to handle. The trick is to develop a style that plays to your strengths. Most handlers use a combination of body language and words to communicate with their dogs.

If you can keep level with your dog most of the time as you move around a course, you will be able to use a great deal of body language. The more you want your dog to work away from you – or to be more independent – the more worthwhile it is investing time in training verbal cues.

Some handling is inherent. In other words, some movements are very likely to be followed by your dog. He will need minimal specific training to react in this way. For example, if you turn your feet to the right, and move in that direction, your dog is very likely to head that way, too. If you slow down a lot, he is likely to slow as well.

Some inherent behaviours are useful and can be utilised by handlers. Other inherent behaviours make life more difficult. For example, imagine you need to continue running into a position, even as your dog needs to decelerate and turn. It will take a good level of training for your dog to override his natural desire to mimic your acceleration, and contradict those cues with his own behaviour.

This is where handling crosses over from inherent mimicry and into skill deployment. It is therefore essential to train your skills first (in other words, teach your dog his foundation behaviours), and handle sequences second – once these skills are learnt. The better your dog's skills, the easier it will be for you to handle him.

HANDLING QUESTIONS

What is a cross?

When you do a cross, you switch your dog from one side of you to the other. Doing a cross influences your dog's choice of lead leg. When your dog is on his right lead, it is efficient and natural for him to turn right. When he's on his left lead, it is efficient and natural for him to turn left.

Generally, dogs will instinctively lead on the leg to turn towards you. This means that if you are on your dog's right side he is very likely to travel on the lead to turn right (unless you are cueing a rear cross at that moment). If you are on your dog's left side he will usually be leading to turn left.

There are three types of cross: front, blind and rear.

What is a blind cross?

This is where you get ahead and exchange your dog from one side of you to the other, *while facing away from him*. For a moment during the cross, you will be 'blind' to your dog.

What is a front cross?

This is where you get ahead and exchange your dog from one side of you to the other, *while facing him*. For a moment during the cross, your front will face your dog.

Bind cross: Although you are facing away from your dog, your change of arm clearly indicates the dog's line of travel.

Front cross: The change of arm should be as smooth as possible so the visual cues are easy to follow

What is a rear cross?

This is where you are *behind your dog when he turns away from you* and switches from one side of you to the other.

So long as I can get ahead I can do a front or blind cross. How do I choose which one to do?

Here are some general principles which will help you decide:

- Front crosses often cue greater deceleration than blind crosses.

Rear cross: As the name suggests, you are positioned behind your dog when you cue a rear cross.

- Front crosses can result in tighter turns; blind crosses can result in looser turns.
- Front crosses often force you, as a handler, to slow down more than blind crosses.

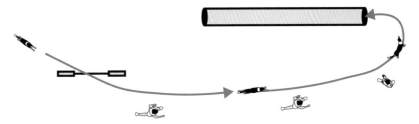

Rear crosses are also useful when you want to keep your dog on the 'off' side of you. For example, if your dog could turn loosely and, by staying on the 'off' side of him, you are able to squeeze him on to the fastest line. In this sequence, see how having your dog on the other side could see him flank out a little, maybe putting the off-course tunnel in his eyeline for a moment?

Should I only do rear crosses when I can't get ahead to do a front or blind?

- Rear crosses are invaluable for situations where you are behind your dog and need him to turn away from you.

What is a ketschker?

This is a move which helps you to get your dog to turn tightly round a wing. To carry out this move, you do a front cross immediately followed by a blind cross. It's all squashed up together and feels like one, quick move, with the dog ending up on the same side of you as he started.

Ketschker: This move is often used on jumps when the dog does a wing wrap. It helps to keep the dog's line tight through the turn.

What is a pivot?

This is a simple move. You turn in the same direction as your dog, and keep him on the same side of you the entire time. You just turn a circle.

Pivot: This move involves turning a circle.

Which is your on-arm?

Your on-arm is the arm closest to your dog at any particular time.

The on-arm, nearest the dog, is also referred to as the drive arm as this will generally indicate your dog's line of travel. The off-arm, furthest from the dog, is only used for specific handling moves.

Which is your off-arm?

Your off-arm is the arm furthest from your dog at any particular time. Your off-arm can be used to cue specific behaviours, such as collection or rear crosses.

What is a serp?

A serp (or serpentine) is commonly thought of as the middle bit of a three-jump snake line.

Serp: With this move you are asking your dog to move in an S-line.

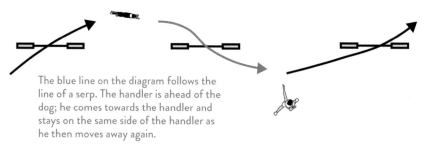

The blue line on the diagram follows the line of a serp. The handler is ahead of the dog; he comes towards the handler and stays on the same side of the handler as he then moves away again.

What is a german?

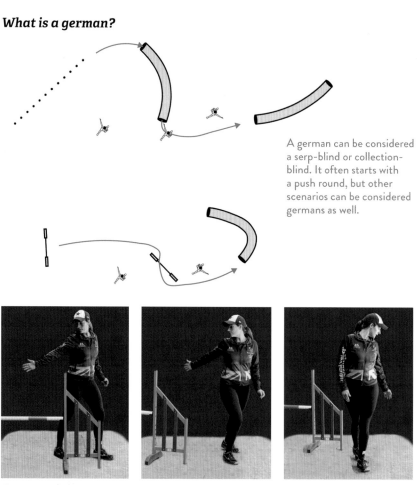

A german can be considered a serp-blind or collection-blind. It often starts with a push round, but other scenarios can be considered germans as well.

German: This move is an extention of the serp with the dog coming from behind to switch sides.

What are flinds, double fronts and double blinds?

A **flind** is a front cross followed by a blind cross.
A **double front** is a front cross followed by another front cross.
A **double blind** is a blind cross followed by another blind cross.

You can use flinds, and other quick combinations of crosses, to subtly adjust the direction in which your dog is heading while you run. Success with these manoeuvres relies on two factors:

1. Keep travelling with your feet as you do the move. Use your upper body separately, so it rotates independently of your feet.

2. Consider exactly where your dog needs the information to exchange from one cross to the next.

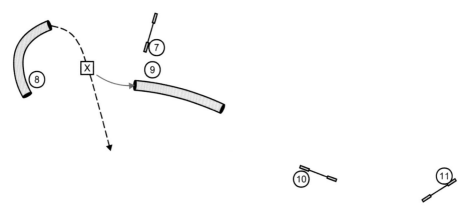

In this exercise, the dog needs to go from one tunnel to the next. The handler needs to keep travelling up the lower side of the second tunnel in order to handle the pull through which follows.

When the dog emerges from the first tunnel, the handler can connect with the dog over their right shoulder. This can be done as a front or blind cross. The effect of this right shoulder connection will be to pull the dog in the direction shown by the dotted line. (If the handler simply kept the dog on their left side at this point there would be a high chance of the dog going off-course, over the back of jump 7). As this connection is made, the handler continues to run forward towards obstacle 9.

Once the dog has adjusted to the position, marked by the X, as a result of the first cross, the handler can then make the second cross. The handler switches sides, via a blind cross, to connect with the dog over their left shoulder. While doing so, the handler continues to travel. This switch will put the dog on the solid line shown, driving correctly into the second tunnel.

Q. I never know which handling option to choose on a course. How do I decide?

What is going on

There is often more than one way to handle a sequence effectively. For example, a sequence of two push rounds could also be two pull throughs. Choosing which course to take in order to achieve the fastest time may come down to how familiar the dog is with each skill, as well as how he is handled. The more you practice, the easier it will be.

Fixing it

Consider how any option you choose will influence where you can get to next on the course. For example, will doing a rear cross in one section force you to rear cross the next section as well because you are now behind your dog?

- Observe handlers you admire course walking. Don't mimic, but do consider why they are making their choices and compare them to yours.

- In training, it's often useful to try options which you consider to be more difficult. In competition, it's better to go with the options that you can readily imagine going well.

- If you haven't got electronic timing, attend a timing training event so you can compare some options accurately.

Q. How do I stop my dog driving into every off-course trap?

What is going on

Be aware of where you are looking. Human psychology can be to look at your dog, and look at where you don't want him to go. That actually tells your dog to go in that direction. Instead, look where you want your dog to be.

Fixing it

Rehearse sequences with traps, and pile on the rewards for running past them. If driving past obvious obstacles is a frequent challenge in training, your dog is more likely to be successful when he encounters traps in the ring.

- Think about how you want your dog to distinguish between staying with you to go past an obstacle and driving into it. What differentiation do you want him to learn? It's probably going to be a combination of where you look, the positioning of your arms and hands, which way your shoulders and feet are facing, and what you are saying.

Q. Why doesn't my dog go ahead of me?

What is going on

Your dog's heritage plays a role in where he will naturally position himself. The rest is down to training. Reward position is usually the most important factor here. Think about this: dogs who love tennis balls rarely have this issue, while dogs who gets treats from the hand commonly do. That doesn't mean you need to use a tennis ball, but it does mean your dog has to be rewarded frequently for driving well ahead of you.

Fixing it

You will need to use a thrown reward, which can easily land far away from you, or a strategically positioned, static reward.

- You need to have clear cues which are, at first, associated with your dog going ahead of you, and can then be used to initiate the behaviour.

Q. Why does my dog flank away from me?

What is going on

If your dog is flanking you, it will feel like you can't get him close to your side and he may turn loosely. Your dog's breed and type play a part but reward position will reinforce or change that. Dogs who love tennis balls often flank, while dogs who most often get treats from the hand, rarely do. Neither reward is better than the other; each has its place.

Fixing it

Your dog should be frequently rewarded for coming into you, even when you are moving. That means a reward from your hand some of the time, for example.

- If your dog is going around jump obstacles there are multiple possible causes. These include the reward position (as above), a fitness, injury or eyesight issue that means he is bailing on jumping, or a lack of understanding that means he feels over-faced.

- The follow my body game (see page 66) may be useful for you to play with your dog.

Q. Why doesn't my dog send away from me?

What is going on

This can be similar to the issue described in **Why doesn't my dog go ahead of me?** (see page 163). It can also be a result of a lack of commitment training (see page 62).

Fixing it

You may benefit by revisiting some individual skills and working on your handling as follows:

- Position yourself at a greater distance from the obstacle to which you are sending your dog. Make sure he is rewarded well away from you, for completion of the obstacle.

- Start to leave earlier, once your dog has been cued to do the behaviour.

- Your dog will send better when you are strategic about your movement on a course (see follow my body, page 66).

- When you are working around tunnels it's especially important to be strategic about your movement. As obvious as it sounds, bear in mind that your dog can't see you in a tunnel. Any movement you make while your dog is in a tunnel is obsolete as handling information. If you want to use your body language to cue something after a tunnel, you need to signal it either just before you see your dog go in the tunnel, or just after you see him emerge.

- Equally, if you need to do something with your body which is unhelpful in terms of the information it conveys to your dog, make the most of the time when your dog can't see you.

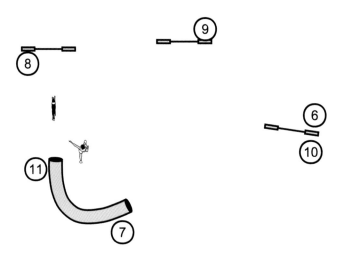

Imagine that in this sequence you wanted to make a blind cross after jump 9. To do so, your dog needs to send away to jump 8. Although it might be easy to get up close to 8 while your dog is in the tunnel, it would be advantageous to do the opposite. If you wait at the tunnel exit for your dog to emerge, you can then show momentum towards 8 by running towards it, without getting right up to that jump. Your movement will help your dog to commit to 8 even when your handling position is relatively far back from the jump, meaning you have plenty of time to cut across to do the blind after 9.

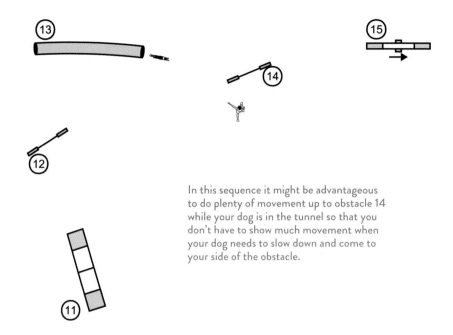

In this sequence it might be advantageous to do plenty of movement up to obstacle 14 while your dog is in the tunnel so that you don't have to show much movement when your dog needs to slow down and come to your side of the obstacle.

Q. Why is my dog stopping, spinning and barking at me during sequences?

What is going on

Your dog is frustrated by your lack of timely information, and it may be that the positioning of your reward is at fault. Don't discount the possibility of physical issues.

Fixing it

Work simpler sequences with a trainer who can help you plan carefully.

- Your dog is not looking to drive ahead of you for a reward so you need to build more value for this behaviour. He needs to believe that going to the reward is far better than the behaviour of spinning/barking, which may have become habitual.

- Reward positioning, and timing, will be key – the reward needs to land, or be visible, well forward of you. Your dog needs to consistently see the reward as he commits to the last obstacle you are sequencing, before he has turned to engage with you in any way.
- Your dog is struggling physically. Consult a canine health professional.

Q. Why doesn't my dog wait in competition, although he does in training?

What is going on

This is similar to the issue relating to stop contacts (see **Why are my stop contacts good in training and not at a show?** (page 146), and you will need to adopt the same policy to get consistent behaviour from your dog.

Your dog is generally over-aroused in a show environment; the loss of his wait criteria is just one manifestation of his inability to manage the increase in stress and excitement. Typically, other behaviours weaken in line with this. He may generally appear more wound up at competition. He may be more likely to knock poles or to bark. He may display reactivity or over-excitement in the run up to his turn in the ring.

Fixing it

Your focus should be on generally reducing your dog's arousal both on a daily basis and, eventually, specifically in a show environment. You need to work on this before you re-attempt success in the ring. A behaviourist or trainer may be helpful. Create a strategy for taking your dog from your vehicle to the ring in a way that prepares him for running, without elevating his arousal. Increase the self-control behaviours your dog performs on a daily basis, as well as at a showground. Make those behaviours valuable to your dog. Be aware that many physical issues can also cause over-arousal.

What is going on

Your dog feels insecure in a show environment and the issue with his wait is not the only evidence of his emotional state. He may show signs such as having his ears further back, and his tail lower down, than normal, and he may look around warily.

Fixing it

Work on your dog's general comfort around anything which seems to trigger this – it could be the presence of other dogs, certain noises, and so on. A behaviourist or trainer may be able to help. Depending on the severity, your dog may need a break from agility or from competitions. You may, with care, be able to increase exposure to the source of his discomfort at training, provided you can do so while maintaining and building his confidence. Reducing day-to-day stressors in his life may be crucial.

What is going on

You tend to associate the movement of your body with your 'verbal' release cue so your dog has learned an incorrect behaviour.

Fixing it

Watch some videos of you, and your dog, doing start lines. Mute the sound. Is it possible to tell, with the sound off, when you release your dog? If it is, then your movement is the release cue rather than your verbal cue. You are, inadvertently, teaching your dog to watch you closely and to mimic your body language. This means that when you move your dog will want to come with you instead of waiting, and he will be unclear when he is expected to release. Focus on keeping your body constant while you release your dog so that the only thing that he can possibly interpret as a release cue is your verbal one. Video your sessions so you can check on your body language.

What is going on

You are inconsistent in show environments compared to how you are in training. When you are training, you have a clear strategy for what to do if your dog's start-line performance is not what you want. In the ring, you feel the pressure of others watching and of taking up the judge's time. Plus you want to get a clear round, so a pre-emptive release – which you wouldn't allow in training – is ignored in the ring. Either way, your behaviour in the ring is different to your behaviour at training. Your dog mimics you – his behaviour in the ring is different to his behaviour at training.

Fixing it

Decide on a strategy which you are happy to adopt across both training and competition. Write down your plan. Now stick to this criteria – both at training and at competition. It will take a while to change the behaviour you accidentally created in the ring, but it is achievable. It may be easier if you start by going to simulated competitions so that you can rehearse your in-ring behaviours in a more relaxed environment.

Q. My dog's jumping style seems to be getting worse. Why?

What is going on

It's not always easy to determine a reason straight off, so be prepared for it to take time and effort to uncover a cause. Behaviours such as stuttering or gathering pre take-off, incorrect take-off position (too early or too late), asymmetry on turns, extra strides on push rounds or pull throughs, pole knocking, inability to turn, and so on, may all have a physical as well as a training cause.

Linda Mecklenburg has published some interesting information regarding what is called Early Take-off Syndrome. It is thought that taking off too soon for a jump can be caused by eyesight problems in dogs.

Fixing it

Any time you see deterioration in performance, get some input from a canine health professional.

- Take videos of your dog's behaviour, ideally in slow motion. History of injury, rather than current injury, can also affect jump style.

- Once you really have ruled out a physical cause, you can start to consider whether there is a mental (i.e. training) cause for the jumping issue.

- Heavy poles can hurt your dog's toes when he hits them and affect his jump style longer term.

- Your dog may have lost fitness, rather than be injured. Or he may need a skill-set revisited.

- Rewards and verbals can also affect jump style. Some dogs learn to take off as soon as their handler says "go," for example. Other dogs launch when they see or anticipate their reward being thrown.

HANDLING WITH EASE

Handling has a lot in common with dancing. During your course walk, you choreograph your moves. In the countdown to your run, you rehearse those moves. The aim is for the choreography, and planning, to result in a faultless performance between you and your partner.

The more readily you can perform each of your moves, the easier handling will be for you. Here are some ideas to help you improve.

Smooth mover

- Write down all the handling moves you want to improve on. So you might write down: "front cross, blind cross, ketschker..." and so on.

- Working without your dog, ask someone else to shout out each move, one at a time, in random order.

- When you hear the move, perform it as quickly as you can. Imagine your dog in your mind's eye, and envisage an obstacle or two if necessary.

- See how quick you can make your response. The less thinking time the better!

Crossing over

Any time you need to make a cross on a course, you can choose from a front, blind or rear. However, you may find that your partnership is stronger at one move than another. Set yourself the task at training of running a whole sequence using just one type of cross – be it front, blind or rear. Repeat over a few sessions, then switch to the next option and so on. This can really push you to get better at the crosses you are avoiding so that, eventually, you and your dog are brilliant at all of them.

Watch and learn

Feel like you don't look the part? Feel stilted or abrupt? Or just not competent at a particular move?

- Make a list of the moves you want to improve.

- Make a list of three handlers you really admire.

- Watch videos of those handlers running courses. Each time you see one of the moves you wrote down, pause, rewind and re-watch it several times. Then try imitating what they are doing.

Chapter Ten

TRAINING & COMPETING

*"The principle is competing against yourself.
It's about self-improvement, about being better than
you were the day before."*

Steve Young

Agility gives you the opportunity to attend a wide range of training events and competitions. It's a chance to make new friends, travel and open yourself up to new experiences.

Who Should I Go To For Training?

To get the best results, train regularly with an experienced trainer who has recently competed at a good level in agility. Look for someone who makes training fun for you, and your dog, and also makes you work hard. It may help to find a social and support network through the training – for example, by attending classes with like-minded people.

Most trainers welcome their students going to other trainers periodically – for example attending training days, seminars and camps. There is also lots of online agility training. Take a look at the websites of some experienced trainers you know, or have heard of, or have a browse on social media. The beauty of online training is that you can train with an internationally acclaimed trainer, no matter where you are in the world.

Think of trainers as people to give you ideas and guidance. No matter who you train with, be prepared to put time and effort into homework in between sessions to get fantastic results.

How To Get The Best From A Training Event

- Anticipate your dog's needs. It could be water, a wee or needing some food midway through to keep blood sugar levels up. Plan ahead and pack accordingly.

- Before training, decide what attitude you are going to adopt:

  - The learning-style attitude. "I will push just beyond what we can currently do, even if it means 'failure,' so that my dog and I learn. I may try things I know we can't quite do so that I can get advice and help."

    This attitude can help you progress and develop.

Or

  - The competing-style attitude. "I will focus on doing what we can already do well. I will help my dog as much as I can so that we have a high chance of going clear".

    This attitude can be useful in the run up to a key competition or when one or both of you needs a confidence boost.

- Prepare mentally before it is your turn to run. Figure out your 'running order' so you know when to do your warm up. Just as you would at a competition, rehearse in your mind what you are going to do when you run.

- You know your dog's skills better than anyone. You know if you have trained commitment on a wing wrap from a distance, or not. You know if your dog has a great understanding of weave entry behaviours, or not. Maybe on your first attempt you need to break down a sequence or reward a skill. Perfect! Run it by the trainer first. Most trainers will be delighted if you take responsibility for your dog succeeding.

- If you can't get your head around a manoeuvre, ask the trainer to watch you rehearse it without your dog.

- If it goes 'wrong,' focus on your dog's experience. When possible, reward. Did your dog try, even if the result wasn't quite what you wanted? It is often handling that creates an error. If your dog follows your incorrect cues, continue with the sequence as if nothing happened or reward him first and then pause to get help with how to improve.

- Stay in the moment. You need to be aware of your dog from the moment you begin until you are ready to reward him. Avoid getting distracted and deciding you want to re-walk a section, or ask a question. If you need to do something like that, make sure your dog is on his lead and being looked after, or is otherwise relaxed and knows he can switch off for the time being.

- It can be hard for you to perform at your best on a training day. There might be someone in the group you don't get on with, or maybe you feel a little nervous of the trainer. The same is true for your dog. He is in a different environment. The kit looks different. The context is different. There might be a dog he isn't so keen on. Be prepared to relax your demands in that environment. For example, if your dog happily jumps 45cm (18in) and sometimes jumps 50cm (20in), start on 45cm or 40cm. You can always raise the height. If your start-line wait is a work in progress, begin with a wrap around a wing or a restrain, and only introduce the wait behaviour later in the session when you are ready to concentrate on it and reward it.

- You might come across sequences which you feel are above your level. Walk them carefully and with great attention to the trainer's advice. Think about which bits are hard for your dog. Are there skills in the sequence you haven't trained yet? Break the sequence down and reward small sections. Be realistic about how much you can both achieve in a short space of time. Make a note of the things you need to go away and teach to make the sequence more manageable for the future.

- You might come across sequences which you feel are below your level. Consider pushing yourself to do options you might otherwise avoid. Work a rear cross instead of a blind. Or choose a push round german instead of a pull through. Ask the trainer if you need some tips on how to make it tougher.

- The trainer has set you a sequence for inspiration. This doesn't mean you have 'failed' if you haven't nailed all the obstacles in a row. Getting a clear round in training is irrelevant. The aim is for you, and your dog, to go away as a slightly better partnership than when you arrived – and with work to take home with you.

- Watch. Watch the dogs: their different movement patterns, their interaction with their handlers. Watch the handlers: their body language, their verbal timing… You can learn so much from observation.

- Take notes during the session. This might include useful feedback points, things to work on, plus insights relating to what you have done or seen.

- If you can give a genuine compliment to a fellow pupil, it will be much appreciated. Everyone is in the same boat.

- Agility is constantly evolving. Stay open to change and development, especially if it takes you out of your comfort zone.

- Enjoy the journey. Value the time you are spending with your dog, with your friends, doing a sport you love.

- Stay strong and stay kind to yourself. You are there, you are trying – nice one!

COMPETITIONS

Competitions are fun. They provide an opportunity to create memories with your dog, to celebrate your hard work, as well as the hard work of others. You have the chance to catch up with friends and make new ones. It pays to be strategic about competitions so you can set yourself up for success.

TRANSITION TO COMPETITION

Approach competitions in a gradual, incremental way. The challenges you both face at trials should be manageable and achievable for your current skill level. Most partnerships benefit from training at a higher level to that which they face in competition. Shows are a more demanding environment for both of you.

Any behaviour your dog can do in his home training venue should be solidly proofed before you attempt it in a trial situation. It is much harder for a dog to do a behaviour in the distracting surroundings of a competition. For example, before asking your dog to weave at a competition, he should be consistently weaving with ease mid-sequence in training. Ideally, he would have weaved in multiple different training environments, using many different sets of weaves, before you ask him to do so in a competition.

Competing at the top level is exhilarating – and nerve-wracking – for both you and your dog.

COUNTDOWN TO COMPETITION TIPS

- Ask friends to act as 'judges' and ring party members.

- Take part in training days at unfamiliar venues. Your dog can learn to generalise equipment. He will start to recognise a tunnel regardless of what colour it is, no matter which sandbags surround it, and so on.

- During training, work some longer sequences. Facing 20 obstacles in competition? Work 25 in training. Remembering and working fewer will feel easy by comparison.

- Work on start-lines with other dogs, and other people, near your dog's position. Work sequences with other dogs training and playing nearby.

- Take your dog to some competitions in which he isn't entered. Work on bringing him near or around the rings, in a way that makes the experience enjoyable. Also rehearse bringing him to the level of arousal you would like for a competition run. That might mean loose lead walking and rewarding calm, relaxed behaviours. Or it might mean getting him fired up and doing a quick succession of tricks on cue.

- Practise engaging your dog with his reward in a show environment.

- Practise your dog's start-line wait behaviour and other self-control games in a show environment.

- Work some training sessions using your competition routine including your warm ups, your start line and your end-of-run reward routine. As you do so, imagine that you really are at a competition. Think about how you will feel and how you will behave.

- Hire other venues with friends. Your dog will develop a better ability to ignore the distractions that come with each new place. You can also rehearse how you want to behave in an environment that differs from the norm.

- Attend train-in-the-ring type events with a show environment. Focus on being consistent so your dog learns that your criteria is the same, regardless of the location and atmosphere.

- Familiarise your dog with running on different surfaces, such as grass, sand-based surfaces and artificial grass.

COURSE WALKING TIPS

How to get the best from those golden minutes

- Before walking, decide your objective. Is it to get the fastest possible time? To train your stop contacts? To go clear?

- If you get a course map beforehand, have a look at it and make a rough plan of line options and handling possibilities. Avoid firm decisions. You will be better to fully determine these once the course is set up. It won't always be a precise replica of what was on paper. Plus, courses can feel different when you walk them.

- Take your dog's safety seriously. Is the tunnel fastened securely? Are the pegs securing the weaves out of the way of your dog's feet? Is the line you intend to work on to the dog-walk safe?

- When you have located the numbers, look for the possible line options for your dog. For example, on any wing wrap there are at least two ways the dog could correctly navigate the jump. Decide on the line you want your dog to run before making choices of how you intend to handle.

- If you are unsure which of two possible routes on a course will be quickest, consider two factors: distance and angle-of-turn. Travelling further takes longer. Turning more is slower. Make sure you consider the entry and exit of a scenario, rather than just thinking of the line on a single obstacle.

- Worried about a bit of the course? Think of a time when you have handled something similar and it's gone well. Recall it with as much detail as you can, then revisit the section that's bothering you.

- Take a moment to determine the fastest possible start location for your dog, i.e. where you will position him in his wait. Your choice of set up location can often have a significant influence on the opening sequence. What can your dog see?

- Think about what is in your dog's line of vision all the way around the course. When he's nearing the end of the tunnel, can he see the weave entry or only the off-course jump?

- Walk the course until you are able to think at least two or three obstacles ahead. Do you know which section of the course comes after the dog-walk, without needing to look up and check?

- Once you are firming up your plan, walk the course while imagining your dog is running it with you. Think about your timing in relationship to him. As you see him driving into the tunnel, are you already moving off down the line of jumps? As you release the seesaw, are you giving your weave cue straight away?

- Sometimes there is a long gap between when you walk a course and when you run, so you may need to prepare for your run with a memory top-up. Develop a strategy for what works well for you. Will you rehearse your plan in your head as you countdown to your run? Will you couple this with watching some other handlers work the course? Will you actively move around a small area and practise your cues?

- Try out your course walking strategies in a training environment to check they work for you. It can be helpful at training to limit your course walking to a specific period of time – for example, six minutes for a 20-obstacle sequence. This can help mimic the pressure and focus of a competition environment.

PERFORMING AT YOUR BEST

Setting goals can help you make your dreams become actionable, achievable plans. Goals can also help you prepare and strategise for the long term.

Decide on your priority competitions for a year or so ahead. Then determine your competition and training strategy based on those priorities. Think about what steps you need to take between now and then to be able to walk into the ring feeling that you and your dog are as fit as you can be, that your training and handling is up to scratch, and that you are both mentally ready.

TIPS FOR PREPARING FOR PRIORITY COMPETITIONS

- Work your dog on the surface on which he will be competing.
- Refine specific behaviours in the run up. For instance, has your seesaw criteria become shaky in the ring? Perfect it in training. Then consider treating competitions that are a lower priority as seesaw practice.
- Find previous courses by the judge who will be officiating and look for trends you can set up and tackle in advance.
- Talk to your canine health professional about how you can best prepare your dog so that he reaches peak fitness at the optimal time.
- Look at results from previous competitions to help you make a game plan. Is it the kind of competition where you need to be tactical and put in multiple clears? Or do previous results suggest nothing but top speed and an all-out performance will cut it?
- Talk to someone who's done the competition before – ask for their tips.
- Attend competitions which have elements in common with the one you are focusing on.

- Watch videos of the event from previous years.

- Familiarise yourself with how the competition will work practically. Get to know the schedule: the order in which you will be running, when you will be course walking and how long you get to do so, where you can keep an eye on the results, etc.

- In training, you will tend to work on making your runs super smooth. But remember in a trial, it isn't over till it's over. Even if part of the run gets a little shaky and doesn't go as you planned, never be afraid to wing it!

- At training, you may be constantly testing and proofing your behaviours. But in competition, where you can afford to support your dog, don't be afraid to do so. For example, you could decelerate on the approach to the weaves, or you could travel a little further forward as your dog approaches a spread jump. You may benefit from rehearsing the attitude you will need in the ring in some training sessions.

- Do some mental preparation before the event. Imagine you are at the event; see yourself there and feeling at your absolute best. You are confident and calm as you course walk, during the countdown to your run, and as you head out to the start-line.

- Ask someone who can provide the practical and emotional support that best suits you to act as your groom at the event. It may help to practise with this support role in a less pressured environment beforehand. Discuss in advance what you want them to do – and not do – to best benefit you.

What are the big international championships?

There are many annual international agility championships. The most prestigious are the European Open and the Agility World Championships. They feature national teams and individuals from around the world – most have qualified to be there via a rigorous selection process.

The European Open is held every summer in Europe. It is open to pedigrees and non-pedigrees and is run under FCI rules.

The FCI Agility World Championships is an annual competition open to pedigree dogs registered with the FCI. It takes place in autumn.

Some of the other well-known competitions are IFCS, IMCA and WAO. These championships are open to pedigrees and non-pedigrees. IMCA is run in conjunction with PAWC, a special paragility championship open to handlers with a range of physical impairments.

There are also breed-specific competitions such as the Border Collie Classic, big events such as the Hungarian Open, and events for juniors such as the European Open Juniors.

It's always worth looking up courses from top international championships, as well as checking out videos posted by the winners online.

Never be afraid to aim high and consider building an international championship into your future goals. Begin by finding out about the qualifying events in your country and go along and watch, so you know what standard you need to meet first.

What is it like competing at an international championship?

Competitive – the top places are usually separated by tiny fractions of a second. At many of these events there may be 60 or 70 clear rounds, so every split second counts.

Exhausting – the adrenaline, the early nights and the long days can make for a full-on competition.

Professional – many of the top partnerships dedicate an awful lot of time, passion, sweat and money into producing their best efforts. As much as it is fun, there is a great deal of professionalism.

Tough – the courses vary and, of course, they are unpredictable, but you are guaranteed to see some super-tough challenges at speed.

Exciting – whether you go as a spectator, or a competitor, you will see some of the world's best agility. You are bound to finish feeling enthused, inspired and motivated to get training!

Ever-changing – agility is evolving rapidly, and this is reflected nowhere more than at international championships.

Chapter Eleven

YES I CAN!

"A trophy carries dust. Memories last forever."

Mary Lou Retton

Agility gets you outside. It gets you moving. It gets you and your dog working together. Agility brings you friends and adventures away from your everyday routine.

For 30 precious seconds you are focused solely on you and your dog. All you hear are your own words. All you feel is the way your dog is responding. Agility is meditation mixed with an adrenaline rush.

HANDLER FITNESS

Being physically fit and agile is a big advantage to you as an agility handler. The benefits include: being able to get into and out of positions on a course, having enough breath to give all your verbal cues, reduced risk of injury, and being able to do multiple runs without tiring. Another big plus is that learning how to enhance your own fitness helps you understand how to enhance your dog's fitness.

There will always be someone who is fitter and faster than you. Don't compare yourself with others. Measure yourself against your yesterday. No matter how fit, or unfit you feel, you will benefit by getting someone on board who can help you improve. A strength and conditioning coach can give you a targeted programme to build on your strengths and reduce your weaknesses. They will know how much you can push yourself safely, and what work you need to do to achieve your goals. They can also advise you on your warm up, your cool down and on your nutrition.

Look after yourself as well as your dog. If you have niggles or injuries consult a doctor and get a health professional, such as a physiotherapist, to help you. If you are free of issues, keep it that way. Prevention is better than cure. Regular check-ups and maintenance therapies, such as massage, can be really beneficial. Remember, the better you understand your own physicality, the easier it will be to help your canine athlete.

You are part of a team so your fitness is a key ingredient.

HAVE I GOT WHAT IT TAKES?

You can tell yourself that you're too old or not good enough. You can tell yourself that you don't have the time or don't have all the kit. The truth is, it's down to you. The fire is inside you if you are ready to let it out. Don't let it be *you* who stops you.

Take responsibility. You have an opportunity. To make your dreams become your reality. To make it work. To make it happen. To give your dog such great skills that you can beat that person who can run quicker than you. That person who is younger than you. That has a faster dog than yours.

Nothing worth doing is easy. Nothing worth fighting for will leap out and hand itself to you on a plate. You have to go out and get it. It takes hard work. It takes effort. Can you do it? Sure. Have you got what it takes? Absolutely.

In 2012 I turned up to the Team GB try-outs for a bit of experience. My dog, Hayly, had only recently qualified for championship level. In those days, at the end of the try-outs the top eight large dogs overall qualified by default. We came seventh.

A few months later I found myself on a coach on the way to Sweden to represent my country. I was surrounded by people I had only ever heard of before; people I had watched run in national finals. I felt like everyone else knew what they were doing. Surely someone was going to find me out as a fraud? Surely everyone knew I wasn't really good enough to be on the team?

On the way out, I stopped at a bookshop and bought a book on sports psychology. I read it as we travelled through Germany and up into Sweden. It didn't transform my mind-set overnight, but it was the first step in the right direction. Since then, I have put lots of time and effort into my mental game.

I have learnt you don't have to know everything. You don't have to have all the answers. The way you feel is okay. Being nervous is normal. Feeling inadequate is expected. Fear is fine. Your job is to try.

IT'S NORMAL TO NOT FEEL GREAT ALL OF THE TIME

It's easy to get caught up when it isn't going well. Easy to start wondering why you have such bad luck. Easy to feel like you'll never get round a course.

There will be times when you will want to pack it in. Everyone feels like that sometimes. There will be moments when nothing goes your way. When luck is not on your side. When not trying is safer. When not going for it means not risking screwing up. When giving up is easier.

Those who succeed at agility are not those who have never met challenges. They are the ones who got up and tried again. And again. And again.

You are not going to come first every time. You will meet elimination after elimination. You might screw up time after time at training. You might come across people who don't believe you can do it. People who doubt you. You might get injured.

Obstacles along the way are a certainty. Expect to meet them. The only thing that matters is whether you let them stop you, or whether you see them as signposts, marking the way to your success.

A great competition run or a fantastic training session can make me feel on top of the world. Like nothing can touch me. I remember winning the British Open at Crufts a few years ago and feeling on a rush for days afterwards. Endlessly re-watching a video of my run. Walking on clouds.

But a year or so before that I was a breath away from winning Olympia when I caused my dog to have a refusal on the last jump. We had the fastest time, the best run and lost it all in that one tiny moment. My heart sank like a stone and I mentally beat myself up for my error for some time to come.

Agility can be an elevator. Emotionally, it's always going up and down. Over the years, I have gradually learnt how to take the rough with the smooth. Like everything, it takes practice but it's worth doing.

FAILURE

Your dog will not be upset if your handling eliminates him. He won't care at all. He's not reading the numbers; he's reading your body language and listening to your voice. If you don't let on that the course you ran wasn't the one the judge set, he will never know. The choice is always yours.

It's easy to be afraid to fail. To see it as shameful. Some people don't even like to use the word because it's considered bad – "failing".

In agility, failure is inevitable some of the time. Failure is useful. It's necessary. When you fail you learn. Failure gives you a chance to not make the same mistake too many more times.

In competition you are statistically likely to have way more eliminations than clean runs. Lucky you – those are a massive opportunity for learning. As for training – well that's controlled failure. It's not always going to go right. It can't.

Expect failure. Embrace failure. Greet failure with pleasure. With excitement. It means you are making progress.

HOW DO I BECOME MENTALLY STRONGER?

- Consider how your trainers make you feel. Go back to the trainers who get the best from both you and your dog.

- Surround yourself with people who have the attitude you want to have. Let into your life the people who believe in your hard work and in the partnership you share with your dog.

- Not everyone will root for you all of the time. On your journey there may be people who are jealous of you. There may be doubters. Some may criticise your choices. That is to be expected. Those people are on their own journeys. Don't be afraid to let some

Work on your mental game to build inner strength and confidence.

people go, or only socialise with them outside of agility. Prioritise the happiness of your dog and you.

- Do you feel like resilience and mental fortitude don't come naturally to you? That's fine. There was a time when a front cross wasn't natural to you either. But you practised. And you practised again. And now doing a front cross seems easy. Be prepared to put time and effort in to improving your mental strength. You don't teach your dog to weave and then never touch that skill again. You keep at it. Your mind can change and develop, just like your body.

- It is human nature to dwell on what's gone wrong; so challenge that with the following strategy. Keep a notepad or a memo on your phone, and after each competition or big training event, fill out the following:

  - One thing I did really well was...

  - One thing my dog did brilliantly was...

  - The best thing someone said to me was...

  - My most enjoyable moment was...

- It is natural to look ahead to what you want to achieve. Remember to celebrate how far you have come, too. Once a year, write down:

  - Three things we couldn't do this time last year, which we can now...

  - My most fun agility moment of the last year has been...

  - The two top things we have achieved in the last year are...

- Tie in happy days off with competitions or training events. Is your trial a few hours away from home? Head there the day before and visit a local attraction. Or persuade some friends to go early too, and just hang out.

- Get online and browse for sports psychology books, audiobooks and videos. Buy some of the ones that take your fancy – maybe the biography of a famous athlete, or a video of hints and advice from a renowned coach.

Trust your dog, and believe in yourself...

- Check out online forums which focus on the mental side of things. On social media you can find groups especially for agility competitors who share ways to improve their mental game.

- Video footage, plus constructive and well-timed feedback from experienced friends and trainers can be useful. When mistakes happen, make a quick note of what you need to work on. Keep your notes somewhere you can check when you go training. Writing down the plan to fix a mistake can help your mind-set become one of action, and stop you dwelling on it.

- When runs go well, replay the video (the real one or the one in your head) again and again. Remember every beautiful cue, every fabulous step you took. Marvel at your brilliance.

- Visualisation can be as useful as real-life practice. Use all your senses to visualise a run in real time. At first, you might find it easier to rehearse this by visualising a previous run that went well. Progress to following up course walking by visualising the run you intend to do on that course. Replay the visualisation in your head, until what you see is exactly what you want to see.

- Goals can be wonderful to sharpen your mind and help you determine practical short-term steps towards improvement. Just remember to love the process, too. Enjoy the everyday steps you are sharing with your dog. In the end, that matters just as much as, if not more than, the outcome.

POSTFACE

Agility matters to you, and so it should – having a competitive attitude can be more than just good, it can be great. Be proud to be up for doing your best! Couple your competitive spirit with a love for your dog and an oath to put him first. Keep your journey together full of fun for the two of you – you both deserve it. You will have a partnership to remember far longer than any dog's agility career can last.